"In the hands of other writers, economics has long been known as 'the dismal science.' But when you read John Tamny you come to *love* economics—because he draws from so many fun and fascinating sources, from the Beatles to Xbox, to make it come alive. Best of all, *The End of Work* pierces through all the gloom and doom surrounding current trends of automation and artificial intelligence to advance a *positive* vision for the future of American workers. It rests on something called Tamny's Law, and all smart people will want to read this book to know what that is."

—**James Rosen,** author of *The Strong Man: John Mitchell and the Secrets of Watergate* and *Cheney One on One*

"John Tamny's *The End of Work* is the answer for everyone who dreads Mondays. In this entertaining book, he shows how passion is becoming the path to a paycheck. The future of work is bright!"

—**John Mackey,** CEO of Whole Foods

"Professional video game players, video game coaches, *NFL Insiders*? John Tamny's exciting book about the explosion of jobs that don't feel at all like work will resonate with those fearful about the future. It's going to be glorious."

—**Adam Schefter,** ESPN NFL Insider

"The United States is where the world's ambitious have long come to make their mark. John Tamny shows why. There are so many things that make America great, but arguably its best attribute is that its freedom correlates with more and more people showing up to work each day with joy in their hearts."

—**José Andrés,** Chef/Owner, ThinkFoodGroup and Founder, World Central Kitchen

"Robust economic growth frees us from the burden of jobs that require little skill, are not satisfying, and leave most people facing Monday with dread. As robots replace humans in certain kinds of jobs, new, impossible-to-foresee jobs will be created, and fewer and fewer people will be going to 'work.' As John Tamny reminds us, they'll be pursuing their passions."

—**Bill Walton,** Chairman of Rush River Entertainment
and host of *The Bill Walton Show*

THE END OF WORK

THE END OF WORK

WHY YOUR PASSION CAN BECOME YOUR JOB

JOHN TAMNY

REGNERY GATEWAY

Regnery Gateway™ is a trademark of Salem Communications Holding Corporation

Regnery® is a registered trademark of Salem Communications Holding Corporation

Cataloging-in-Publication data on file with the Library of Congress

ISBN 978-1-62157-777-5

Published in the United States by
Regnery Gateway
An imprint of Regnery Publishing
A Division of Salem Media Group
300 New Jersey Ave NW
Washington, DC 20001
www.RegneryGateway.com

Manufactured in the United States of America

10 9 8 7 6 5 4 3 2 1

Books are available in quantity for promotional or premium use. For information on discounts and terms, please visit our website: www.Regnery.com.

For Claire,
may you never know what
it is to dread Mondays.

CONTENTS

Andy Kessler

What do you do? We all get asked this at meetings, interviews, cocktail parties, everywhere. It's almost as if the person asking is trying to put you in some cubby and figure out how you tick by branding you as a certain type of person, which magically unlocks the mystery to your personality. But these days, there are so many interesting, bizarre, and confusing answers to "What do you do?" that it's hard to put someone into a predefined box anymore.

Depending on who is asking and my mood at the time, I've got lots of choice responses. Nowadays I say that I'm a writer. Or an author if I think someone might actually read one of my books. But I've also been a Wall Street analyst, an investment banker (briefly, until I found out you had to be nice to people) a venture capitalist, and for many years I ran a hedge fund. But I'm an engineer by training and used to design chips, install computer systems, run networks, and write code. I've even written a few video games. Oh yeah, and I've been a waiter, a car hop at a root beer stand, and even a baker's assistant. (Actually, I washed pans, but he once let me put poppy seeds onto buns.) I'm likely to answer with any one of these or at least try to work them into a conversation.

But as I look back, I don't consider any of them to be a job. The Navy used to run recruiting ads on TV with the tag line delivered in a deep booming voice, "It's not just a job, it's an adventure." That's how I've always felt. I got a paycheck, but it almost never felt like work. It felt like, well, an adventure. New ideas to explore every day, new puzzles to solve, new concepts to explore, new things to learn. What's not to like? I'm not a morning person, but because it didn't feel like work, it felt like going to Disneyland. I was mentally ready (almost) every morning to start work.

Anyway, if it ever did feel like work, because I had a boss who was a jerk, I would quit and figure out something else to do. If you sum up all the jobs you've ever had, it's a career. Looking back on my so-called career, I see it as a game of pinball, bouncing from one bumper to another until I found something interesting enough and lucrative enough and free enough of annoying bosses to make me stick around for a while and figure it out.

Of course, when I look back at all this, it scares the crap out of me. At any point I could have ended up at a dead end or fired or unemployed. It wasn't the typical career path for the 1970s and 80s: doctor, lawyer, accountant, management, public service, military, or some other regimented and often narrow path. But my wandering worked.

I often wonder why. Really, why? By all means, coming out of central New Jersey in the fog of the 1970s, I should have ended up working in a factory. I did spend years getting an engineering education, so maybe I was more likely to end up at IBM perfecting some widget and wearing a white short-sleeve shirt, clocking in at precisely 8:11 a.m. and out at 4:42 p.m., with a twenty-two-minute lunch. Or maybe I'd have ended up crunching numbers wearing green eyeshades, only to be replaced by an electronic calculator that was faster and more accurate.

But I didn't. Why? Was I privileged? Heck no. Lucky? Maybe. Right place, right time? Perhaps.

Though few saw it at the time, technology was completely changing work in the United States—how it was organized and how the idea of labor evolved into human capital, with brains being more important than brawn.

I'm sure any decent management consultant could construct a labor stack, with factory and food-service jobs, not requiring all that much brain power on the bottom; logistics, with a little brain and a little brawn, a little higher up the stack; management, which means dealing with people; and pure design, almost exclusively thinking, topping it off.

As cheap microprocessors and cheap memory have been followed by fast networking and cloud computing, technology has relentlessly advanced and allowed more and more jobs to move up the stack, leaving labor to less-developed countries. Sure, there is still manufacturing in the United States, but it tends to be higher-value products, complex machinery, and pharmaceuticals rather than clothes and consumer goods. So many jobs have moved up the stack that the United States is predominantly a service economy, meaning more and more workers are removed from grunge and sweat and turmoil and get to think for a living. That's the secret to having a job that doesn't feel like a job.

Years ago I wrote a piece on this for the *Wall Street Journal* opinion page and convinced them the title should be "We Think, They Sweat." The iPhone and its software are designed in the United States in air-conditioned offices, and the only way you would sweat would be if you came in too quickly from kiteboarding on the San Francisco Bay and sweated through the pits of your Vineyard Vines shirt. iPhones are, of course, manufactured in China. We think and design. They sweat by running machinery and staring into microscopes and moving boxes around in the most complex logistics dance ever known to mankind. And our jobs reflect this.

I think two things happened that affected me. First, technology came along to bring faster and easier computing closer to all of us. Mainframe computers gave way to workstations and then to personal computers, laptops, smartphones, and tablets. The saying in Silicon Valley is that intelligence moves out to the edge of the network. Closer to you and me. We use it to think on a higher plain, moving around concepts instead of boxes and earth.

The second thing that happened was that databases came along to allow money that was formerly managed by the sclerotic trust departments of stuffy Victorian banks to be sliced and diced into mutual funds and hedge funds and eventually exchange traded funds. Wall Street completely transforms. But this financial transformation also allowed risk capital to fund innovation, changing Silicon Valley from sleepy orchards into the innovation machine it is today.

Years ago, I accompanied my sons' middle school class on a tour of an automobile factory in Fremont, California. General Motors and Toyota had a joint venture they called New United Motor Manufacturing, Inc., or NUMMI, which was supposed to be a showcase of the future of automobile production. It eventually failed, and Tesla now uses the space to make electric cars. But back then, they had the coolest tours. After a few minutes in a conference room fitting all of us with hard hats for protection, they loaded us twenty at a time onto little trams that drove around the factory, carefully staying on a path of dotted lines.

It was loud, and the pace of the assembly line was faster than I expected. The tour was as frenetic as "Mr. Toad's Wild Ride" at Disneyland. Every once in a while, you would hear classical music playing. The assembly line would stop and there would be concerned looks by some and smiles on the faces of workers on the line. We learned that anyone with a problem could pull a cord, stopping the line and causing music to play. This was an innovation by the Japanese (especially the classical music) to minimize defects. Better to stop the line and correct the problem cheaply in the factory than have a wheel fall off a vehicle after fifteen thousand miles.

After years of investing in Silicon Valley tech companies and seeing incredible innovation every day, I stifled a chuckle when I saw that pulling a cord and playing music was the auto industry's idea of innovation. Eventually, the tour found itself at the most complex stage of manufacturing: the installation of the engine, which had been assembled in Japan and shipped to California. One man, who looked about sixty but boasted impressively ripped muscles, seemed to be in charge of this step. It was explained that with overtime, this guy, who was close to retirement, was making more than a hundred thousand dollars a year. Our tour leader pulled up close to him and asked into the microphone, "Any advice for the kids on the tour today?" With sweat dripping off his head and a partial grimace on his face, he muttered, "Stay in school."

Technology wraps the economy in a fabric of productivity. Dress yourself in it. It's about doing more with less. It's about replacing older, less interesting, sweaty jobs with machines and creating more and better jobs requiring human capital. No one wants to believe this. The fear today is that robots will take everyone's job, requiring the government to issue checks to all its citizens in the form of Universal Basic Income. This is hooey.

Machines augment human beings and slowly but surely replace jobs at the lower end of the stack. Buttered buns are made by machines. Airline tickets are sorted in databases rather than by human beings. Artificial intelligence can implement image recognition and sort photographs and tag videos better than any person can. That's why the race up the stack toward higher and higher levels of human capital and thinking is so important.

The race is never over. Human beings will always need to improve themselves and increase their capacity to think. But along the way, the drudgery of low-end jobs is exported to developing countries that need it or is eliminated altogether. We are left with jobs that don't feel like jobs, careers that don't feel like careers. Our productive lives become a blessing rather than a burden. And every one of us contributes, not just some self-selected elite. Wealth gets created for a wider and wider swath of workers, rather than distributed by policy wonks.

Once you think, any job is possible. And it won't feel like a job. Get ready for a life of adventure.

Andy Kessler, the co-founder and former president of Velocity Capital Management, is the author of *Eat People: And Other Unapologetic Rules for Game-Changing Entrepreneurs.*

*"Man's work begins with his job; his profession. Having a
vocation is something of a miracle, like falling in love."*[1]
—Hyman Rickover

I n the fall of 2014, my wife and I attended a Fleetwood Mac concert
in Washington, D.C. Calculating that after decades of global popularity the band members were closer to retirement age than to
their musical prime, we decided that we should see them live while we
could. But watching them on a massive screen from our seats in the
back of the auditorium, it was clear that they were having too much
fun to call it quits anytime soon.

Mick Fleetwood's joy as he thrashed his drum kit was astonishing.
Even more striking was the intense happiness on the face of Lindsey
Buckingham. Here was an amazingly talented guitarist doing what
he plainly loved to do. You couldn't separate his hard work and his
passion.

A concert tour is grueling work. There's a reason that musicians
train for months before hitting the road. It's brutal out there. As the
Rolling Stones guitarist Keith Richards recalls in his memoir, *Life*,
sickness from exhaustion on stage was the norm: "How many times
I've turned round behind the amplifiers and chucked up, you wouldn't
believe! Mick pukes behind the stage, Ronnie pukes behind the stage
too."[2] The members of Fleetwood Mac, though not as frenetic on stage
as the Stones, work feverishly to the delight of their millions of fans.

Buckingham earns his living making music, but that night it was apparent that this hard-working guitarist was hardly working. The passion revealed on his face was a reminder that when a man pursues what he's good at and what he loves, he's not really working.

Buckingham's glee reminded me of a story my father told me about a buddy at the U.S. Naval Academy who showed up sick one day at rowing practice. At most other schools he would have been sent back to the dorm to rest, but the Navy coach told him to get dressed. Rather than miss practice, he would sit in the bow and watch the rest of the crew row.

As the ailing midshipman observed his teammates in action, it was apparent which ones were working hard and which ones were going through the motions. After practice, he remarked to the coach how eye-opening the experience had been, and from that day the coach required each rower to watch a practice from the same vantage point. You can't hide laziness. It will be exposed sooner or later.

In an early nineties television ad, Spike Lee asked Michael Jordon whether it was the shoes, the socks, the haircut, or the vicious dunks that made him the best basketball player in the universe. But as Jordan will tell you, hard work and practice made him the greatest. He would practice with the same intensity he brought to a game, so "when the game comes, there's nothing I haven't already practiced. It's a routine."[3]

The same goes for future Hall of Famer Kobe Bryant—it was all about the work. His former Los Angeles Lakers teammate Ronny Turiaf observed that Bryant "was always in the facility by himself, working out in the gym or practicing on the court. He was always the first one to show up. I don't know when he slept."[4] Jordan and Bryant revealed their love of their chosen profession by working like demons to perfect their game.

Warren Buffett, on the other hand, could never do what they did. By his own admission, the billionaire investor would starve if he had to make a living playing basketball. If we lived in a sports-based economy, he writes, "I would be a flop. You could supply me with the world's best instruction, and I could endlessly strive to improve my skills. But, alas, on the gridiron or basketball court I would never command even a minimum wage."[5] In fact, if football and basketball had been Buffett's only choice of jobs, he probably would have been thought of as lazy as well as a flop.

Fortunately for Buffet, he had the opportunity to become an investor, and he's the Michael Jordan of allocating capital. Half a century ago, Buffett purchased a struggling textile mill, which he turned into the collection of blue-chip companies known today as Berkshire Hathaway.[6] A lousy basketball player, Buffett has few peers when it comes to recognizing the world's best companies. If you'd had the good fortune to buy a thousand dollars' worth of Berkshire stock back in 1964 and held onto it, that stock would be worth $11.6 million today.[7]

Like Buckingham, Jordan, and Bryant, he searched for and found his passion. As Buffett himself once said, "In the world of business, the people who are the most successful are those who are doing what they love."[8] Buffett may be an outlier when it comes to talent and brains, but that's advice that everyone should take to heart.

But what about you? Are you lazy? You've probably thought so; maybe said so to others. And others may have said it about you. Maybe that's why you bought this book. It's a fair bet that there have been times when you've just gone through the motions, and you've known it. It's easy to pinpoint days of light effort because after a day of not giving it your all, you don't feel good about yourself.

"Blood, sweat, and tears" *matter.* Far from being the cause of emotional pain, they're the path to happiness. Some people have a naturally sunny temperament, but no one is born with *happiness.* And no one can bestow happiness on you. It's the result of developing your talents. Work itself is the surest path to happiness.

But work alone isn't enough, as a visit to a poor country where people work unceasingly just to survive would attest. Biting your lip and soldiering on in your miserable job isn't the only way to avoid laziness. You'll never be consistently productive if you loathe your surroundings, your job, or both. You're human, after all!

The central message of this book is that *you're not lazy, you're simply in the wrong job*. And there's nothing wrong with that. Successful people will tell you that success springs from the pursuit of all kinds of work—with lots of failure in the process—on the way to finding what has you excited on Sunday nights, as opposed to what has you depressed.

As long as you're doing work that you're not interested in, you'll never be a consistently hard worker, and you'll never maximize your talents. Worst of all, odds are you'll never achieve the happiness that could be yours if you pursued what you're good at.

The essential question, then, is what are your skills? What work have you done that brought you joy, that earned you praise and admiration? If you see yourself as aimless, it's likely that you're working out of obligation, not passion.

If going to work is painful, ask yourself what it pains you *not* to be doing. What would you be doing if you didn't have to earn a living? That's probably the vocation that makes sense.

Of course, matching work with passion, making what it pains you not to be doing your professional occupation, is a luxury. It cannot happen without prosperity. But where prosperity is the rule, more people will be able to express their talents and intelligence in the workplace. It's simply the case that a rising tide lifts all boats. The freer people are to earn as much as they can and keep it, the more likely it is that everyone will have the opportunity to make a living from his own unique skills and intelligence.

Don't misunderstand me—doing what you love will not be fun all the time. Nothing worthwhile is ever easy. Pursuing your passion, you surely will encounter obstacles and criticism. And it's not the work of a day: you will have to work long and hard to discover and develop your talent.

But here's the great news: as the United States and the rest of the world advance economically, rising prosperity makes it increasingly likely that you will have the opportunity to do what you love. And the greatest gift of prosperity, beyond freedom from material want, is work that is engaging, absorbing, fulfilling—work that doesn't *feel* like work.

I'm not trying to teach you how to work hard. I'm saying that people work hard when their work engages their talent and passion. You are not lazy or stupid. Whatever you've been told and whatever you believe about yourself, you have within you the work ethic, intelligence, and charisma that you marvel at in others. What's missing is the kind of work that inspires the heroic effort of which you're capable. I'm going to show you that that work is within your grasp and how to recognize it. Truly, the end of work is near.

CHAPTER ONE

Why College Football Players Should Major in College Football

"As a coach, I know I have to start with smart players.
It might not have been so important in past eras,
but today we're asking players to do so much and
to know so many schemes. Without basic intelligence,
they simply can't play."[1]
—Hall of Fame football coach Bill Walsh

"I honestly have no idea what I would do without it."[2]
—Christian McCaffrey, 2015 Heisman Trophy runner-up,
Stanford All-American, 2017 first-round draft pick
by the Carolina Panthers, on football

To illustrate the financial significance of being taken in the first round of the National Football League draft, *Sports Illustrated* compared the fortunes of Melvin Gordon of the San Diego Chargers and Landon Collins of the New York Giants. The fifteenth player picked in 2015, Gordon received a contract that included a $10.7 million guarantee. By contrast, Collins, the first player picked in the second round, was guaranteed $6.2 million less. To put that in perspective, the article pointed out that "the average U.S. engineer will make a little over half that [$6.2 million] during an entire working lifetime."[3]

It's good to be an NFL player these days. The average salary is $2.1 million annually, and the league minimum is $435,000.[4]

Needless to say, few people make that kind of money right out of college—not even engineers. Indeed, being an NFL player is a great gig if you can get it.

Even better than the salary average is the trajectory of pay. The NFL's annual revenues of $10 billion put it on par with several countries. The league gets $5 billion a year for the rights to televise its games, $1–2 billion in sponsorships, and another $2 billion from ticket sales. It also reportedly earns $1 billion from licensing and merchandizing sales.[5] As revenues grow, so do players' salaries, which make the earnings of doctors, lawyers, and CEOs look trifling by comparison.

There are threats to the NFL's prosperity, of course: cable TV "cord cutters," concerns about the game's violence and injuries, and the political fallout from players' comportment during the National Anthem. What's important here is that market signals belie the pessimism. As Kurt Badenhausen reminded *Forbes* readers in 2017 amid all the worry about the league's health, "The Dallas Cowboys were the only NFL team worth $2 billion five years ago. Now all but five of the NFL's thirty-two teams are worth at least $2 billion (the Buffalo Bills bring up the rear at $1.6 billion)."[6] Team valuations help explain the surge in salaries. The mean salary of the top 5 percent of U.S. earners increased 31.7 percent from 2000 to 2016. Over that same period, the mean NFL salary increased 205 percent.[7]

Assuming continued growth in the game's popularity, the "wealth gap" between NFL athletes and the rest of us will keep growing. The problem for the rest of us is that few of us have the intelligence—yes, the *intelligence*—to play football on the professional level. Not only do most of us lack the physical requirements, but it's a fair bet that we lack the necessary mental skills.

Mike Holmgren is likely headed to the NFL's Hall of Fame. After coaching two Green Bay Packers teams to the Super Bowl in the 1990s, winning one of them, he proceeded to turn around the fortunes of the hapless Seattle Seahawks in his native state of Washington, taking them to their first Super Bowl in 2005. Their loss to the Pittsburgh Steelers in a game marred by more than a few lousy calls by the referees did not diminish Holmgren's reputation as one of the greatest offensive minds the sport has ever produced. In particular, he is an expert on the quarterback position. Here's how he described the position that Brian Billick, another Super Bowl-winning coach, calls "the single most difficult position to master in the world of team sports"[8]:

> Say you want to learn Chinese. You go to a class and learn it over a period of years, and you practice speaking it, and pretty soon, after a few years, you can speak Chinese fairly well. Imagine trying to learn something as difficult, an entire system of plays, and taking the knowledge and making decisions on what to call and where to throw, all within split seconds, and doing it with people running at you trying to knock your ass off.[9]

Recalling his rookie year with the Tampa Bay Buccaneers, Jameis Winston—who had won the Heisman Trophy and was the number-one NFL draft pick—says he "had a lot to learn. Coach [Dirk] Koetter threw the entire playbook at me. The different names of the calls, I really had to study those so I didn't mess them up." For example: "Diablo right. H-Ram, 76, F-Chief, X-Hitch. It's a freeze call. I'm trying to get a man zone read off the running back. It's an easy progression. We have a lot of long play calls."[10]

Football, particularly in the NFL, is about so much more than athleticism. In addition to the new language, players have to memorize a playbook the size of the Yellow Pages. Successful NFL players not only are good at the game but love it enough to master it—a staggering task.

Boomer Esiason is known today as a host of CBS's *NFL Today*. He's in the position to be a highly-paid sports commentator, however, because of his success in the 1980s and 90s as a quarterback for the

Cincinnati Bengals and New York Jets. Having led the Bengals to within seconds of a Super Bowl victory over the San Francisco 49ers, he was denied the coveted championship ring by Joe Montana's last-minute ninety-two-yard touchdown drive.

Explaining what a quarterback is up against after breaking the team huddle, Esiason describes a play against the Washington Redskins, then one of the NFL's best teams:

> The Redskins like to shift, and from the 45, they go right into the 46 look, the old Bear defense. And the forty-five-second clock is ticking down, and I don't have much time to get the play off, and we're inside the red zone, second and seven, and I'm thinking all of a sudden, "This is their blitz down. They're coming." So I've got to think of my blitz audibles. I'm in flip formation, I'm in strong backs, they're running eight men up to the line of scrimmage, they're coming.
>
> I go, in a hurry, "2–80, 2 zulu, 2–80, 2 zulu, check 95, check 95, green, green, green! Everybody got it?!" They got it. What we're going to try to do is hit James Brooks on a wide flare to the strong side, thinking Rodney Holman, the tight end, can get out and wall off the inside linebacker who's man-to-man on James Brooks.[11]

Are you starting to regret the times you've booed the QB of your favorite team for a mistake? Esiason goes on to describe the extraordinary preparation leading up to each game:

> [Y]ou have to know every play, every audible, every code word, every single nuance of the game plan, because 60,000 people will be screaming, with three or four million more watching on TV, with every eye on you, and coaches, officials, players all waiting for you, and you hardly being able to hear anything, and the clock ticking down second by

second. I have to get every player in the exact right position with all these things going on around me.

You've got to know what you're doing. It takes years to master it. It took me two and a half years to feel totally comfortable in this stuff. Now, I love it.[12]

When Dak Prescott was quarterback of the Mississippi State Bulldogs, he figured out that field skills were not enough. "I learned...that you win at this position by knowledge, by being ahead of the defense mentally," he told *Sports Illustrated*. His knowledge impressed the Dallas Cowboys' scouts and front office, who concluded that Prescott's football IQ was the highest of the seven signal-callers they interviewed ahead of the draft.[13] He's now the Cowboys' starting quarterback.

Tom Brady might be the best quarterback ever, but not because he's the most athletically gifted. It's his uncanny mind. Charlie Weis, a former offensive coordinator with the Patriots, recalls, "I don't know if I've ever met anyone who reads coverages as quickly and correctly. [When I was there] you could count on one hand the times he saw something incorrectly."[14]

Quarterbacks aren't the only players who need brains. The center, for instance, has to know where every fellow offensive lineman is supposed to be and where every defensive player is lined up in case he needs to alert the offense with a line audible. And Anthony Lynn, a longtime NFL assistant, loads his backs up with *homework*: "Early in the prep week Lynn hands out packets of worksheets, with one page for each play in the game plan. For all running plays, the backs write in the formation, the defensive front and how the concept is blocked. They must draw one dot for the primary read and two dots for the 'second-vision' read, and they must highlight the big alert, if there is one." If that sounds obscure, that's the point. The great players are the *students* of the game. Hall of Fame running back LaDainian Tomlinson told Lynn that "learning how every run is blocked up front made him a better ballcarrier. 'My game went to the next level when I learned what everyone on offense was doing.'"[15]

To the untrained eye, wide receivers simply run crisp routes with great speed. If only. Michael Irvin, the Cowboys' Hall of Fame wide receiver, explains what was going through his mind during a particular play against the Washington Redskins' defensive back Darrell Green. The actual catch was the easy part:

> Look at how much went into that, and look at how many things could have gone wrong. I could have slipped. The pass could have been a split-second late. The pass could have been off to one side. The pass could have been high. If the pass is off, I still get the shit beaten out of me, and all for nothing. It's amazing when you think about it, that so much goes into the catching of one ball. All the timing you build up with the quarterback, all the work you do to build that timing and trust in the offseason.... And it looks so easy. That's the strange thing.[16]

Former wideout Haywood Jeffires adds that "it takes two solid years to learn the system, and three to get out on the field and do something. It's not till your fourth year that most guys are ready to play instinctively."[17]

As difficult as it is for wide receivers to learn the game of professional football, it's even more difficult for the defensive backs covering them. Sure, backpedaling as some of the world's fastest human beings race by you is tough, but it's the mental aspect that's a killer. Tony Dungy, a Hall of Fame coach and former defensive back himself, says, "It's a mental position much more than a physical position."[18]

Imagine preparing to line up across from Larry Fitzgerald or Odell Beckham each week. The film preparation is endless. Rod Woodson, a Hall of Fame defensive back, points out that it wasn't enough for him to be focused on one receiver. He had to understand what the *entire* offense would do.[19] Defensive backs are some of the highest paid players because, like the quarterback, they're staring down the proverbial barrel of a gun every play. They have to make countless reads in a matter of seconds while chasing some incredibly fast people.

Ok, but how difficult can it be for defensive backs at least mentally to outplay Patriots tight end Rob Gronkowski? Can someone with his reputation and nickname ("Gronk") actually be smart? Actually, yes.

No less an authority than Bill Belichick has observed that the position Gronk plays at an All-Pro level "is, probably after quarterback, the hardest position to play in our offense. That's the guy who does all the *formationing*. The running back is usually in the backfield. The receivers are receivers. But the tight ends could be in their tight end location, they could be in the backfield, they could be flexed. They could be in the wide position. To formation the defense, those are the guys you're going to move. It's moving the tight ends that changes the defensive deployment." Belichick continues, "Rob is a versatile athlete, but he's also a versatile guy mentally. He can handle a lot of different assignments. Some guys can't. Either they mentally can't do it, or it's just too much and their game slows down. They don't play to the same skill set you see athletically because they're thinking too much. That's not the case with Rob."[20]

Let's not forget that Gronk is doing all this with more than seventy thousand fans looking on, millions more watching on television, and similarly smart and physically gifted players looking to hurt him. In short, Gronk is passing an exceedingly difficult test each Sunday.

The NFL is both tough and *cerebral*. The adjustment from college-level play to the pros is extraordinarily difficult, and the disparity between the collegiate and pro games continues to grow. As then-University of Houston head football coach Tom Herman remarked in 2016, "I do catch NFL games every now and again, and it doesn't remind me of anything that I watch when breaking down opponents or watching college games on TV. It's completely different."[21] Stephen Jones, the Dallas Cowboys' COO, agrees: "[I]n my 25 years with the

NFL, I've never seen a larger disparity between the college and pro games."[22]

Greg A. Bedard, writing in *Sports Illustrated*, describes college games as "high-scoring affairs ruled by simple schemes on both sides of the ball and even simpler techniques." Sundays, by contrast, "are a chess match":

> Quarterbacks bark out complicated play calls in the huddle and then change them at the line. Defenses bluff in and out of different looks and then bring an unorthodox blitz with press-man coverage. The offensive line has to execute perfectly timed double teams from three-point stances, or the running game doesn't go anywhere.[23]

With the college and pro games increasingly different, the old expectation that it would take college players two years to adjust to the NFL has been extended to three. "[C]ollege football's rule that restricts meeting and practice time to 20 hours a week" limits players' readiness for the new game, writes Bedard, making the draft "even more of a crapshoot than before."[24]

Because the NFL is so demanding, young men who are good enough to merit an expensive college football scholarship should be *encouraged* to major in college football, cultivating the physicality and intelligence required for a spot on an NFL roster—a spot, by the way, that any given player is exceedingly unlikely to attain.

"*What's that?*" you ask. Am I really suggesting that college football players should major in their sport even though most players in even the best programs don't make it to the pros? Why would anyone recommend that players devote all their college years to athletics when the odds of a pro career are so low? It's a good question, but also kind of a silly one.

At a typical American university, countless business majors are focusing their efforts on business classes. Only a tiny fraction, however, will be offered a job upon graduation at Goldman Sachs or a top hedge fund. Other students are pre-med, but probably a smaller fraction will end up at Massachusetts General Hospital or the Mayo Clinic. Communications majors number in the thousands, but how many will wind up reading news at NBC or ABC? How many English majors will ever rate a professorship at a top school or a reporter's job at the *New York Times*? How many will write a book that gains substantial notice?

It's odd, isn't it, that the academic pursuits of the average college student don't raise eyebrows, but if a young man talented enough to earn a scholarship wants to work feverishly at a sport he's incredibly good at in pursuit of entry-level earnings that will dwarf those of more traditional majors, he is dismissed as delusional and shortsighted.

Sure, you say, a kid's dreams of Goldman Sachs or the CEO's suite may be farfetched, but those business and engineering majors will be trained for all manner of professional work. Maybe so, but let's not forget that the nature of work is changing all the time. In our constantly evolving economy, the jobs of today rarely predict the jobs of tomorrow. Millions of people who work all day on a computer weren't trained in college for what they do now. How much of what *you* learned in school is relevant to the work you do today?

The University of Southern California, Notre Dame, and the University of Miami have produced the most—and best—NFL players. USC and Notre Dame claim twelve Hall of Famers each, with the next-closest school having only nine in the Hall. Alabama and Florida State are also in the top ten.[25] Now, the NFL odds of any given player matriculating at one of these "football factories" are still low. But that doesn't mean a scholarship recipient should spend more time in business and English classes than in perfecting the athletic skills that brought him there.

Indeed, what will open more doors for a college athlete after the cheering stops, a résumé that includes participation on a top team—perhaps an interception, tackle, or touchdown in a major game—or an A in English or marketing? Given alumni's enthusiasm for their alma mater's gridiron glory, an average player—or even a benchwarmer—probably has better post-graduation employment prospects than a student who has good grades but is otherwise invisible. Moreover, the kind of guy who can survive and thrive for four years under Nick Saban, Urban Meyer, or Brian Kelly brings something to his job that a classroom-savvy student lacks. A capacity for excruciatingly hard work and rigorous discipline tends to catch an employer's eye.

But apart from that, remember that prosperity and economic evolution produce professional opportunities that don't seem like "work." A century and a half ago, the only career most people could look forward to was farming. How energetic and intelligent might you appear if all you could expect in life was daily toil in the fields?

Fortunately, technological innovations made it possible for fewer people to produce more food. More to the point, prosperity made it possible for young men to leave the family farm in pursuit of the more rewarding opportunities that always emerge from growth. Today, something similar is happening for those who view football as life's ultimate pursuit. Simply put, you no longer need to play professionally in order to earn a good living in football.

NFL coaches who were star players themselves are the exception, not the rule. Most head coaches got there the hard way. Doing something they loved, they put in brutally long hours over many years in pursuit of the ultimate football prize that doesn't involve being on the field.

Waived by the 49ers and the Cowboys after playing tight end at Brigham Young University, Brian Billick worked as a lowly assistant coach for his high school and (simultaneously) for Redlands University, served as a PR assistant for the 49ers, and toiled as an assistant at Utah State, San Diego State, and Stanford before he reached the NFL. Then he spent years as tight ends' coach and offensive coordinator for the Minnesota Vikings before finally getting his chance as head coach of the Baltimore Ravens, whom he led to victory in Super Bowl XXXV.[26] The work was endless, Billick recalls. "I know of few people in any other profession who work from late July until January without a single day off."[27]

The work may be endless, but imagine getting to put in long hours doing something that you're passionate about and reaching the highest heights. Rare is the football coach who possesses a Super Bowl ring.

NFL head coaches are paid handsomely for all that work. Sean Payton of the New Orleans Saints is the highest paid at $8 million per season. The Seattle Seahawks' Pete Carroll earns a similar amount, while the Patriots' Bill Belichick pulls in $7.5 million. Even coaches who haven't gotten to a Super Bowl, like the Cowboys' Jason Garrett, earn more than $5 million annually.[28]

The pay for assistant coaching isn't as well publicized, but as far back as 2004 Washington Redskins defensive assistant Gregg Williams earned $1.8 million annually.[29] General managers usually earn in the millions, vice presidents in the $400,000 range, and directors of college scouting are said to earn $275,000 and above. Their assistants tend to be at the bottom end of six figures.[30]

Coaching at the college level can be dazzlingly remunerative as well. Going back to 2005, the average annual pay for head coaches at 119 major college football schools was $950,000. Nowadays that's chump change. Numerous college assistants out-earn that dated average today. Only one head coach earned as much as $3 million in 2006 (Bob Stoops of Oklahoma), but in 2016 there were at least thirty-six coaches earning at or above the $3 million mark.[31] As of 2015, the average pay for head coaches at 128 major colleges was $2 million.[32] At the top of the compensation pyramid are Michigan's Jim Harbaugh ($7 million) and Ohio State's Urban Meyer ($6.5 million), while Nick Saban, whose Alabama Crimson Tide seems to be the permanent national champion, signed a $65 million contract extension in 2017 that averaged out to $11.25 million per season.[33] After the 2017 season, Texas A&M inked a ten-year, $75 million contract with former Florida State coach Jimbo Fisher, every dollar of which was guaranteed.[34]

Coaches get to the top by surrounding themselves with capable assistants. And they pay them very well. Saban's offensive coordinator Brian Daboll (since departed for the NFL) earned $1.2 million in 2017, defensive head Jeremy Pruitt took home $1.4 million, and outside linebackers coach Tosh Lupoi $950,000.[35]

The average assistant coaching salary in the Southeastern Conference, generally regarded as college football's best, is $447,000,[36] but the number is constantly changing because of feverish bidding. In January 2018, Louisiana State signed defensive coordinator Dave Aranda to a four-year, $10 million deal.[37] What top head coaches used to be paid is now assistant money.

The impressive pay scales extend beyond the ranks of the powerhouses. The average head coach's salary in the unpretentious Conference USA is $628,000.[38] The average 2015 salary for all assistant coaches in the major college ranks was $245,000.[39] Not "One Percenter" money, but close.

You don't even have to be an expert on football to make money in the sport. If weight training is your passion, you might be courted by some of the best coaches in football if you're really good. Alabama's strength coach, Scott Cochran, after Georgia tried to poach him, was retained with a salary that exceeds $535,000.[40] And he isn't even the highest paid strength coach on the collegiate level. That honor goes to Iowa's Chris Doyle, who signed a contract in 2016 that will pay him $600,000 annually.[41]

With both the NFL and college football booming economically, even high school football is lucrative. In 2016, voters in McKinney, Texas, near Dallas, overwhelmingly approved a $62.8 million, twelve-thousand-seat stadium. Football-crazy voters approved similarly lavish stadiums in the Houston suburb of Katy ($62.5 million) and the Dallas suburb of Allen ($60 million).[42]

High school coaching salaries have risen along with the cost of stadiums. In 2014, four high schools in and around Austin, Texas, paid their coaches more than $100,000 per year, with eleven others earning more than $90,000.[43] In Houston, more than fifteen coaches earned more than $100,000 in 2016,[44] while twenty-three coaches in Georgia hit six figures.[45] Football hotbed Alabama had nine coaches in that exalted bracket in 2017.[46]

A sport that once was remunerative only for the few now offers career possibilities for the many. A sport that requires extraordinary physical gifts combined with keen mental ability no longer must be abandoned upon graduation from high school or college. It makes sense, then, for college football players to major in—yes—*college football*. The game is so popular with the American people—and increasingly the world—that it brings with it high earnings even for those who don't rate an NFL player's contract.

And if the football-focused change their minds, that's fine. The hard work and smarts required for football are preparation for all kinds of careers that aren't related to football. Even better, many colleges now allow scholarship athletes to return to campus if things don't work out on the professional level—or even if they do. As Clemson's director of athletics, Dan Radakovich, wrote in 2015, "We also provide the Tiger Trust, which allows any student-athlete who leaves campus in good academic standing to return on athletic aid to complete his or her degree."[47] In short, if football doesn't work out, former players will be able to finish their degree for free.

Major in college football? Without question. It's a no-brainer.

CHAPTER TWO

Intelligence and Passion Don't Stop at Football

*"If you love the game, then you've already won! You can't
be beat. Because the reality is, a lot of guys don't love it.
When I came here in 1996, I had the butterflies, and then
when I got around everybody, it was like, Oh, I'm fine.
Some of these guys don't love the game. I thought they did.
They don't. It's a job for them. And when something is a
job, you can have success for a week, two weeks, a month,
maybe a year, maybe even two. Then you'll fall. It's inevitable. But if you love it, you can't be stopped. Because when
you love something, you'll always come back to it. You'll
always keep asking questions, and finding answers, and
getting in the gym."*[1]
—Kobe Bryant

*"I don't care if you're a man or a woman, the best thing
about Michael Jordan was his mind for the game."*[2]
—Becky Hammon, San Antonio Spurs assistant coach

No one has ever called the California Institute of Technology a jock school. The tiny university in Pasadena is a Nobel Prize factory, boasting thirty-five laureates among its faculty and alumni. But Caltech does have a basketball team, and in 2008 it managed to steal the head coach of its East Coast rival MIT, Oliver Eslinger.

Perhaps he moved for the weather. It certainly wasn't Caltech's athletic tradition that drew him to Southern California. The Beavers once went twenty-five years without winning a game in the Southern California Intercollegiate Athletic Conference.[3]

Other academically-minded schools occasionally make allowances for certain athletes. Not Caltech. The Beavers' infamous history of losing would make recruiting hard enough, but Eslinger would have to hunt for athletes with the grades and SAT scores to earn admission to a place like … well, Caltech.[4]

Still, life's challenges are what elevate our proverbial game, and Eslinger proved up to the challenge. Searching far and wide for average athletes with excellent grades, he found them in such out-of-the-way places as Wasilla, Alaska, and even Qatar. At the end of the 2010–2011 season, Caltech broke its streak of losses with a 46-45 win over nearby Occidental College. In subsequent years, Caltech even strung together consecutive conference wins.[5]

Eslinger had so changed the culture at Caltech that he started to attract players who were actually good, including a six-foot-four-inch guard by the name of Brent Cahill. Declining an invitation to walk on at the basketball powerhouse UCLA, Cahill told *Sports Illustrated*, "Why would I want to practice four hours a day if I'm not going to the NBA?"[6]

With Caltech grads earning an average of $82,000 a year right out of college, Cahill's choice made sense for him economically. But it made no more sense than the choice of scholarship-worthy basketball players to focus on the activity that most develops their own physical and intellectual intelligence—basketball.

Kobe Bryant, the legendary Los Angeles Laker, was known around the National Basketball Association for his incredibly high basketball IQ. Bryant could see the whole floor, anticipating the moves of his opponents and teammates. Although he skipped college to go straight to the NBA after high school, his education in the game of basketball had just begun.

Bryant already had NBA-level talent when he joined the Lakers in 1996. But as he told his teammate Byron Scott, "I want to be the best player in the league."[7] Endless practice was a huge part of a career that included five NBA championships, but so was study. Lee Jenkins of *Sports Illustrated* wrote that the young Bryant "was cocky but curious. He asked a hundred questions, of teammates but also opponents. He once asked Michael Jordan at a stoppage about the release angle on his fadeaway."[8]

After the 2014–2015 season, Golden State Warriors power forward Draymond Green signed with the team for five years and $82 million. Green has talent so special that if not for his suspension from game five of the 2016 NBA finals versus the Cleveland Cavaliers, the Warriors likely would have hoisted the second of three straight NBA Championship trophies. But what most fans miss is how much Green *studies* in order to be the player he is.

In a pre-season game ahead of the Warriors' recording-breaking seventy-three-win campaign of 2015–2016, Lakers forward Julius Randle "singed" Green with his "go-to-stutter-step move." Green responded by asking a Warriors assistant for every film clip of Randle's move going back to his time at the University of Kentucky. Green told *Sports Illustrated*, "I studied the s— out of that move, and figured out what I needed to do [to] stop it."[9]

At Michigan State, Green "deconstructed Big Ten scouting reports for his teammates."[10] They say he can sniff out the opponents' plays before they run them.[11] He even tries to learn from the WNBA, whose players teach him more about the fundamentals of the sport than his NBA brethren. As he explains it, the women "know how to dribble, how to pivot, how to use the shot fake."[12]

LeBron James and his Cavaliers deprived Green, Steph Curry, and the rest of the Warriors of a second straight championship. James's enormous talent is well known, but it's his basketball intelligence that his teammate Kevin Love raves about. James is a manager on the court, says Love. "You have to understand people and how to deal with them. LeBron is incredibly smart. He knows how to get the best out of us."[13]

Love is not alone in his respect for James's otherworldly intelligence in his chosen line of work. One NBA head coach calls him the "smartest player in our league."[14] Anyone who even sniffs the NBA is an extraordinary athlete. What's unappreciated is that the MVP-level performers are the Warren Buffetts of their profession.

Why *wouldn't* Caltech players want to spend more time working differential equations than practicing basketball? That's what reinforces their skill and brings them happiness and success. At the same time, classroom-smart Caltech players would look pretty hapless on a basketball court with Bryant, Green, and James—and not merely because of the mismatch of athletic gifts. Those masters of basketball know their sport the way Stephen Hawking knows theoretical physics.

If you've got what it takes to make a career in basketball—that is, if you're good enough to rate a collegiate basketball scholarship—it makes sense to pursue it. The money isn't bad. In 2014, the NBA signed a $24 billion, nine-year deal with ESPN/ABC along with TNT to televise its games. In June of 2016, Nike signed an eight-year deal with the NBA to outfit its teams to the tune of more than a billion dollars per year. Coke, Pepsi, and Anheuser-Busch InBev are just a few of the name brands in partnerships with the globally popular league. Thanks to deals like these, not to mention television rights sold to local stations, the NBA is flush with money. This wealth is reflected in the value of individual teams, thirteen of which are worth at least one billion dollars.[15]

As the value of each NBA franchise soars, so does the pay for the league's players. From 1985 to 2016, the average NBA salary rose 80 percent, to $5.2 million per year. These numbers explain the "one and done" phenomenon that has become the rule among top college basketball players. If you're good enough for the NBA, it makes no sense to hang around campus for three more years when the minimum pro salary is more than half a million dollars.

Of course, there are only thirty NBA teams, with rosters limited to fifteen players. Isn't it absurd to plan a basketball career in the face of such impossible odds? Sure, but as global prosperity increases, so does the desire of the world's newly prosperous to be entertained. You don't have to be one of the 450 NBA players to make a living in basketball.

More and more foreign countries are getting professional leagues of their own. Basketball is both internationally popular *and* lucrative. Most professional basketball players outside the United States earn from $1,500 to $20,000 per month, and some of the top European players earn as much as $50,000 per month.[16]

Each year, millions of once desperately poor Chinese join the middle class, and these newly prosperous consumers like basketball. There are now players in the Chinese Basketball Association earning more than a million dollars per year, even though their season has only thirty-eight games.[17] As prosperity takes hold around the world, so will demand for basketball talent. And the story doesn't end there.

The NBA is littered with head coaches earning $5 million or more per year, and a few—like Gregg Popovich of the San Antonio Spurs, Glenn "Doc" Rivers of the Los Angeles Clippers, and Tom Thibodeau of the Minnesota Timberwolves—make more than $10 million.[18] NBA assistant coach salaries are harder to track, but reports indicate that many earn in the high six-figure range.[19]

At the collegiate level, at least thirty-five college head coaches were earning $2 million or more in 2017. Duke's Mike Krzyzewski sat atop the heap as recently as 2016 with a salary of $7.3 million, but by 2017 Louisville's Rick Pitino (before he was fired in a scandal) and Kentucky's John Calipari were pulling in more than $7.4 million.[20] As reporters noted in *USA Today*, "The $2 million coach, once rare in college men's basketball, is becoming routine among the upper-echelon programs."[21] Pay for assistants is also on the rise. Calipari's assistant Kenny Payne earns over $500,000 each year, roughly what he earned as an NBA player in the 1990s.[22]

Basketball's popularity, unlike football's, extends to the women's game too. Draymond Green is surely on to something when he watches the WNBA to learn the fundamentals. Geno Auriemma, head coach of the University of Connecticut's perennial national women's championship team, earns $2.17 million each year. At least two of his counterparts at the other three 2016 Women's Final Four schools weren't doing too badly either. Washington's Mike Neighbors earned $410,000, with Oregon State's Scott Rueck right behind him at $400,000.[23]

The good times in basketball extend to the high school level, even in football-mad Texas. Four boys' coaches and four girls' coaches in San Antonio were earning more than $80,000 annually in 2017.[24] High school baseball coaches are also doing well in San Antonio, where five earn more than $80,000.[25] Something is up. To see what that is, let's turn our attention to the game of baseball.

Michael Lewis's classic book *Moneyball* (2004) depicted the evolution of baseball into a numbers game in which statistics-crunching wonks ran teams like a hedge fund. The Oakland A's general manager Billy Beane and his team of quants revealed that the traditional ways of evaluating players were highly flawed. Readers of box scores and home run counts suddenly looked silly. There was a serious game behind the game that brought to mind Warren Buffett and value investing.

The precursor to *Moneyball* was George F. Will's *Men at Work: The Craft of Baseball*, published in 1990 and the bestselling baseball book of all time.[26] Will explained to Americans how incredibly complicated, precise, and, yes, *cerebral* their national pastime is, drawing readers' attention to the importance of mental ability. Baseball IQ *matters* in a big way. As he explains in the introduction to the twentieth-anniversary edition of *Men at Work*,

> I do not deny that extraordinary (literally: not ordinary) physical ability and natural talent are prerequisites for playing baseball at the major-league level. But neither do I believe

that those gifts are sufficient. The history of baseball is littered with stories of failures by players who thought that
their natural physical endowments would be sufficient.[27]

Men at Work was also the precursor of this book in two important
ways. As Will observes in the same introduction, "The financial
rewards that accrue to athletic excellence are already enormous, and
as our increasingly affluent society increases its leisure time and discretionary income, those rewards will increase."[28] He saw that prosperity would allow more people to pursue "non-traditional" work to meet
the growing demand for entertainment.

Even better, Will pointed out that in an economically advanced
society with rising disposable income, people can pursue passions that
have little to do with their professional work. As he put it, "the writing
of *Men at Work* was not done by a man at work. Nothing that was so
much fun should count as work."[29] Will is fortunate to have been born
in the affluent twentieth century, when men no longer had to spend
nearly every waking hour toiling to survive. "Work" done for fun
became a reality in our wealthy country in the last century. It will
become a global norm in this one.

To give his readers a deeper understanding of baseball, Will
explains various positions by focusing on a particular figure—Oakland's Tony La Russa (manager), the Los Angeles Dodgers' Orel Her-
shiser (pitcher), the San Diego Padres' Tony Gwynn (hitting), and the
Baltimore Orioles' Cal Ripken (fielding). If you read *Men at Work* you
never see the game the same way again.

The manager, writes Will, "is responsible for wringing the last drop
of advantage from situations that will occur in each game. To do this
he must know the abilities his players have revealed in their past per-
formances and he must have similar knowledge of the players in the
opposite dugout."[30] Local scouts, advance scouts, position coaches, and
front office workers keep him supplied with that crucial information.
For example, La Russa's pitching coach, Dave Duncan, briefs him on

Red Sox outfielder Ellis Burks: "Third base, we play him straight. Short-stop, we play him to pull. Second baseman will be up the middle until there's two strikes on him and then we'll move back to straightaway."[31] Will describes his exhaustive game preparation: "Duncan has charts for all balls put in play by particular players off Athletics pitching, a chart for those balls put in play to the infield, a chart for those to the outfield."[32]

La Russa couldn't manage by pure instinct unless he wanted to fail. As Will tells it, his "'instincts' are actually the result of an 'accumulation of baseball information.' They are uses of that information as the basis of decision-making as game situations develop."[33] Baseball, in other words, is not for the stupid.

The late Tony Gwynn understood that. He told Will:

> I just don't feel I'm prepared unless I'm doing what I can to be a little bit smarter, a little bit better, a little bit more pre-pared. I have been brought up in the game to do every little extra thing, get every bit of extra knowledge that can help you get a base hit in a key situation.[34]

Gwynn knew so much about hitting that he could tell from the windup what some pitchers were throwing. His confidence was the fruit of "work done—with batting machines, with videotape—before he gets to the plate. His reaction depends on his analysis of what this particular pitcher does."[35] Gwynn "will look at tapes for hours. He has one tape of each team. Each tape has all his at bats against that team in the season."[36] Gwynn was unquestionably a great athlete; he played baseball *and* basketball at San Diego State. But he was also a remarkably intelligent student of baseball. His physical and mental prowess made him a Hall of Famer with a career batting average of .338 alongside 3,141 hits.

That same kind of baseball intelligence characterizes today's stars too. Consider the Chicago Cubs' outfielder Kyle Schwarber, an indis-pensable member of the 2016 World Series champions. Schwarber is "not going to go into macroeconomics and get an A," says his college roommate Kyle Hart, but "when you get on the baseball field, that kid might as well be Albert Einstein."[37]

If you're hoping to make baseball your life, I've got the same exciting news for you that I had for football and basketball lovers. Combined revenue for Major League Baseball's thirty teams was $8.4 billion in 2015. From 2011 to 2016, team values rose 146 percent on the way to an average of $1.3 billion.[38] And as you might expect, player salaries are rising accordingly. When the 2016 MLB season began, a record 127 players were set to earn more than $10 million per year, while the average Major League salary rose to $4.4 million.[39]

The high pay at baseball's top level is starting to trickle down. The average AAA minor league salary is about $2,100 per month, while some players in the system earn in the $60,000–$70,000 range per season.[40] It's only a matter of time until the pay on the "farm teams" reflects the soaring value of the teams at the top.

Major League Baseball doesn't disclose the salaries of managers, but at least three can claim annual earnings of $5 million—Joe Maddon of the Chicago Cubs, Mike Scioscia of the Los Angeles Angels, and Bruce Bochy of the San Francisco Giants—with several more making a million dollars or more.[41]

As baseball becomes sophisticated, games are more likely to be decided by the slightest advantage in information. This development is raising the profile of coaches, who, as Tom Verducci notes in *Sports Illustrated*, haven't always gotten much respect. Historically, the "first base coach has been held in such low regard that among the many who have filled the job for major and minor league teams are Michigan football coach Jim Harbaugh (for two teams), the Famous Chicken mascot and 7'2" former NBA center Greg Ostertag."[42] Mickey Mantle, an occasional first base coach himself, observed wryly, "There's nothing to worry about out there. Nobody listens to the first base coach anyway. I never did."[43]

The rising fortunes of first base coaches are a reminder that baseball's past is no predictor of the present. Winning in the "Moneyball" era is less about home runs than about getting runners on base and advancing them. Verducci writes:

> Thanks to the proliferation of video and the difficulty of the stolen base, the role of the first base coach has gained greatly in importance, even if much of it remains unfamiliar. Armed with granular intelligence to crack secret codes, the first base coach, not the manager, just might be masterminding your team's running game.[44]

As the coach's role has changed from ceremonial to crucial, his pay has grown accordingly. Nowadays, a first base coach makes between $75,000 and $125,000.[45]

What about the scouts, the guys who fill out the minor league rosters that will eventually determine the look and quality of the majors? Barry Svrluga calls them "baseball nomads," whose "job is filled with tedium: calling coaches for pitching schedules, driving countless miles to high school games, talking with families and friends to learn players' histories, their other interests, their favorite ice cream flavors."[46]

To most people, scouting would be not a job but a sentence. Yet for someone who's baseball-mad, it's a foot in the door. Mike Rizzo was a minor league player who didn't quite have the game to reach the majors, but the growing administrative side of baseball allowed him to remain a part of a sport that he loved. He started as a scout at $11,000 a year—scouts now make about $30,000—and today he's the general manager of the Washington Nationals.

Recalling for Svrluga his traveling days as a scout with another ex-minor leaguer, Kris Kline—now a colleague at the Nationals—Rizzo says, "Neither of us really had any other interests. I often ask him, 'What would you do if you weren't in baseball?' He has no answer for it. I have no answer for it."[47] Rizzo weathered the low pay in the early days pursuing the only thing he cared about, and now he earns $2.5 million a season.[48]

As for Kline, while he's not sitting in the general manager's chair, his work at a lower salary for a thriving team sets him up for a more lucrative future. In addition to his salary, he's now got 1.2 million Marriott points and thirty-five free round trip flights on Southwest Airlines—that's a lot of otherwise expensive vacations. Above all, he's pursuing his passion. "People spend their whole life trying to find the one thing you love doing," says Kline. "I've found it. I don't need to do that."[49]

There are lots of guys like Kline. The Nationals employ more than "1,100 people who never get an at bat or throw a pitch."[50] But they're part of a sport that fascinates them and on a team whose value continues to surge upward. The line about a rising tide lifting all boats isn't a theory. It's reality. The better the elites of baseball do, the more the game can employ thousands more who love it.

Compensation is one of the most powerful market signals. Word of good pay and intangibles tends to travel. Baseball is big business, and it's attracting top-flight people whose talents aren't necessarily athletic. In 2015, the ranks of general managers included graduates of MIT, Stanford, and Amherst (there were *three* Jeffs, actually).[51] *Sports Illustrated* reported in 2016, "Every MLB organization has an analytics team in place to try to figure out what to do with all the data that comes from 2,430 games—roughly 750,000 pitches—a season."[52] And the baseball writer Bob Nightengale has called the Los Angeles Dodgers "Analytic Geek Squad, a group boasting Wall Street résumés, Massachusetts Institute of Technology diplomas, including Ph.D.s."[53]

Today, top athletes and front office executives alike apply their impressive intelligence to a game they're in love with. Gone are the days when most of us had to toil joylessly just to get by. That's the dividend of prosperity.

CHAPTER THREE

Education Isn't Meaningless, But It's Grossly Overrated

> *"The successful conduct of business demands qualities quite*
> *other than those necessary for passing examinations—*
> *even if the examinations deal with subjects bearing on the*
> *work of the position in question."*[1]
> —Ludwig von Mises

In December 1965, the world of popular music changed forever. The Beatles released *Rubber Soul*, introducing to the hypercompetitive music market what became known as the "concept album." Instead of a random mix of hits and filler, the album was a coherent whole to which every piece contributed. Each song on *Rubber Soul* was "seemingly more brilliant than the one before it," writes the pop music historian Kent Hartman.[2] A new standard for music making had been set.

The Beatles were at Capitol Records along with the Beach Boys and throughout those heady days "maintained a friendly rivalry" with the Californians. Brian Wilson, the brilliant leader of the Beach Boys and creator of their sound, was keenly aware of how much the critics loved *Rubber Soul*. As Hartman tells it, he began "to scramble in reevaluation of their own efforts. He wondered how the Beach Boys would even be able to compete."[3]

Wilson's frustration, born of his admiration for the work of the Beatles, speaks to the beauty of competition. In economics they call it free trade. The Beatles' shot across the proverbial bow sent a message to Wilson that if he was going to be taken seriously by critics, peers, and the buying public, he had to have an answer to *Rubber Soul*. Wilson delivered with *Pet Sounds*.

In those days, some bands toured while their creative forces behind them stayed in the studio to make music. Wilson sent the Beach Boys out on tour while he worked on his masterpiece with a group of studio musicians eventually nicknamed the "Wrecking Crew."

Wilson was an "outsourcer," as it were, and the Wrecking Crew were among the best studio musicians in the industry. Wilson brought them together for three months to make what Paul McCartney viewed as "the greatest pop album of all time."[4] The principal musicians on *Pet Sounds* were Hal Blaine, Carol Kaye, and Glen Campbell, with Wilson himself as the maestro orchestrating the Beach Boys' response to *Rubber Soul*.

None of the players involved had a traditional musical education. Wilson was deaf in one ear, and while he grew up in a musical family, his schooling was conventional. A big guy, he played on the football team. But something about music clicked with him. One of the best ways to understand his genius is to listen to "God Only Knows" from *Pet Sounds*, noting the multitude of instruments and what bass player Jerry Ritz called "countermelodies." As Ritz saw it, Wilson combined sounds and melodies in completely new ways.[5]

Drummer Hal Blaine grew up poor in Hartford, Connecticut. There was no extra money lying around to pay for musical instruction, so he learned how to drum by "watching" drummers he admired—"one of the only affordable methods of instruction he could manage."[6]

Guitarist Glen Campbell grew up even poorer in Billstown, Arkansas, passing many a night "lying on his stomach while pressing his fist into his gut, trying to quell the gnawing pangs of hunger."[7] In Campbell's destitute family of twelve, focused as it was on putting food on the table, there was "little emphasis on schooling," and even when Glen made it to class, he "showed little natural interest in sitting behind a wooden desk."[8] Yet music evoked from him another kind of intelligence. As Hartman writes:

> From the time almost anyone could remember, Glen showed a preternatural aptitude for anything to do with a musical instrument. By the age of ten he'd ably learned to pluck notes and strum chords—all by ear, no less—on a cheap five-dollar acoustic guitar that his father purchased for him from the Sears & Roebuck catalog.[9]

Carol Kaye was the daughter of failed musicians whose lack of money led to lots of arguing and ultimately to divorce. For years her mother had put coins in a piggy bank, which she cracked open the day a steel guitar salesman came to the door. The price of the instrument included a few lessons, but it was not until an accomplished guitar teacher heard Carol play (she tagged along with a friend who could afford lessons) that her musical career took off. Recognizing the girl's extraordinary talent, the guitarist offered to teach Kaye if she would *help him* instruct his students.[10]

The creators of *Pet Sounds* were not Juilliard grads, but their skills remind us that passion and talent are more important than classroom instruction. Phil Spector, one of the most prominent producers of the 1960s and a constant presence at Wrecking Crew sessions, did receive a first-rate musical education, but it proved meaningless. He yearned to be a top jazz guitarist, but his teacher told him bluntly,

> No, Phil, in truth, I don't see that for you. You're lacking one thing that a musician absolutely has to have. And that's meter. You don't *feel* when one musical phrase ends and another begins. I'm sorry. But I can't teach you that. I don't know anybody who can.[11]

How lucky, then, that Spector could recognize in others what he himself lacked. No amount of education could make up for Spector's lack of talent. He could hear what sounded good but couldn't play it.

Pet Sounds was a commercial disappointment when it was released, but today, despite the humble credentials of its creators, *Rolling Stone* ranks it the second-best album of all time.

The story of the Beatles is similar. While they came from varied economic circumstances, all were poor by today's standards. None of the Fab Four's families even owned a car.[12]

The poorest was easily Ringo Starr, whose early life was, in the words of the Beatles' biographer Bob Spitz, "a Dickensian chronicle of misfortune."[13] In a world in which education was the "way out," Starr found school "a great and terrifying burden—he felt ostracized there—making it easier just to stay away."[14]

A bout with tuberculosis put him even further behind in school, and he never returned. But in the tuberculosis ward, he developed a knack for the primitive version of "drums" at his disposal: "cotton bobbins to hit on the cabinet next to the bed." Spitz writes:

> There was something familiar in the process, a natural feel to the way he held his hands, the impact of the sticks on the wooden surface, and the colorful patterns that emerged. He didn't just make noise; there was more to it than that, there was a complex range of sounds he could produce just by experimenting with his wrists.[15]

Music would be more than Starr's "way out." It would be his life.

Guitarist George Harrison didn't distinguish himself in the classroom either. Yet he was the first musician to play the wildly complicated sitar on "a major pop recording"—*Rubber Soul*. With no previous training on the instrument, Harrison "worked night and day to try to master its intricacies."[16]

Paul McCartney "picked up instruments the way some people pick up new languages; he had the ear for it, with all the proper accents in place," writes Spitz.[17] As his brother Michael explained, once Paul picked up a guitar, "He was lost. He didn't have time to eat or think about anything else."[18]

Like the other Beatles, John Lennon had no time for school of any kind. He "responded wretchedly to anything structured, and guitar instruction was no exception."[19] By his teens, he was failing his classes, but it was of no consequence to him. As he told a teacher with total conviction, "I'm going to be a rock 'n' roll singer."[20]

So the greatest musical act ever, the Beatles, was composed of four guys who not only had no formal musical training but also couldn't even read a note of music.[21] That's a powerful reminder that education is generally about teaching yesterday's news, while economic and commercial progress is about doing what's not been done before.

There was no school to teach the Beatles how to get to where they wanted to go. And while they had myriad musical influences, the excitement that greeted their arrival on the musical scene indicated something quite original. Again, unteachable.

Another case in point is the Rolling Stones. Keith Richards's mother, Doris, wanted to be an actress or a dancer, but opportunities for that were rare in 1950s England (or anywhere else, for that matter). With the global economy on its back in the aftermath of World War II, there was lots of hard work to be done. So Doris got a job demonstrating washing machines. She was good at it, but her family couldn't even afford the machines she was explaining to others.[22] They also didn't have a record player for much of Richards's early life.[23]

The Richardses didn't have phonograph albums, but Doris was an expert with the "knobs," bringing music into the house through radio, and Keith learned to play his friends' guitars. When he was fifteen, Doris purchased his first guitar—acoustic, since they couldn't afford an electric one. As Richards would point out decades later in his autobiography, "if you want to get to the top, you've got to start at the bottom."[24]

"I've learned everything I know off of records," recalls Richards, a *listener* to music out of economic necessity. "Being able to hear recorded music freed up loads of musicians that couldn't necessarily afford to learn to read or write music." The well-heeled could go to music school or concerts, but as the British economy developed, radio and the proliferation of records made it possible for someone like Richards to get a musical education on the cheap.[25]

In April 1962, Richards sent a letter to his Aunt Patty updating her on his doings and mentioning his encounter with one Mick Jagger at the train station. They'd begun to play music together, and as Richards relayed to his aunt, "Mick is the greatest R&B singer this side of the Atlantic and I don't mean maybe."[26] A band was starting to take shape, its members filled with passion but none of them educated in music.

A pattern is emerging here. It seems no degree is required to make a fortune in music. Of course, the odds of achieving success on the level of the Beach Boys, the Beatles, or the Rolling Stones are similar to those of making it in the NFL. It's crazy, isn't it, to urge someone to skip traditional education on the microscopic chance that he'll be the next Keith Richards. That's a reasonable objection, but again, it misses something important.

An evolving and prosperous economy makes it more likely that someone will have the *chance* to develop his talents. There's no guarantee that because you love to play the guitar and sing you'll become a star. But because of our economic evolution, you have a much greater chance today of making a living with music than ever before.

When Keith Richards and the Rolling Stones were starting out, it was a big deal to get to make music at all. It was one thing to perform live, and the Stones did a lot of that, but studio time was expensive. When the Stones were on the outside of the music business looking in, Richards recalls, "It was nearly impossible to get into a recording studio. It's bizarre that now anybody can make a record anywhere and put it on the internet. Then it was like leaping over the moon. A mere dream."[27]

Today, as Richards says, anyone can make a record. And musical acts have the worldwide web as an inexpensive way to project their sounds globally.

Justin Bieber was a twelve-year-old nobody from Stratford, Ontario, when he began posting videos of himself singing on YouTube. The views picked up steam, and Bieber was discovered by the talent manager Scooter Braun. A bidding war broke out, and soon the boy sensation had a recording contract.[28]

The XL Recordings label discovered Adele after her friend posted a demo on MySpace in 2006. Carly Rae Jepsen's modest fame was limited to Canada until Bieber tweeted about the catchy nature of "Call Me Maybe" in 2011.[29]

None of this is to say that what Bieber, Adele, and Jepsen achieved was easy, or even likely. But it is to say that the musically passionate should feel more comfortable about shunning the traditional "get an education, then find a job" career track that is the historical norm. In an increasingly prosperous global economy, more people can confidently focus on what they're best at, then work feverishly—including working for a living on the side—to amplify those skills. And it will be a lot of work.

Brian Wilson labored over *Pet Sounds* for "three grueling months" of work, usually "from seven at night until early the next morning." Blaine regularly slept at the studio, while "Birthdays and anniversaries were forgotten, school plays were missed, and in several instances marriages sadly ended."[30]

With the Beatles, the music was all-consuming. Radio Luxembourg broadcasts barely reached Liverpool, but its "rock 'n' roll" music captivated John Lennon, who had no interest in the dated offerings on BBC Radio. Those broadcasts were his *education*, and he took it seriously. Furthermore, he didn't have the luxury of buying music on the cheap to listen to repeatedly. Records were costly, and a young man of modest means had to rely on radio broadcasts from the Continent.[31]

Once the Beatles were big enough to tour, they would perform at night after working all day, spending the hours on the tour bus writing song after song.[32] As their biographer explains, "Their peers all had day jobs; the Beatles had never even thought seriously about punching a clock. It was only ever music, only the band, *only the Beatles*. There were no other options. This was their life's work."[33]

So it was for the Rolling Stones, who endured "constant, unmovable" poverty on their road to fame.[34] Richards's diary from the period is filled with notes about their "gigs" and what they were paid, if anything: "January 21, Ealing Club, 0, January 22, Flamingo, 0, February 1, Red Lion, £1 10s. At least we got a gig. As long as you've got a gig, life is wonderful."[35]

Although the Rolling Stones later developed an impressive party reputation, they couldn't afford those luxuries when they were on the other side of stardom. If they weren't performing, they were working:

> We needed to work together, we needed to rehearse, we needed to listen to music, we needed to do what we wanted to do. It was a mania. Benedictines had nothing on us. Anybody that strayed from the nest to get laid, or try to get laid, was a traitor. You were supposed to spend all of your waking hours studying Jimmy Reed, Muddy Waters, Little Walter, Howlin' Wolf, Robert Johnson. That was your gig.[36]

The point is that if your work is an expression of your talent and intelligence, it may be hard but it's not drudgery. You excel at something, perhaps many things. The goal should be to identify what that is and match what you love with extreme effort. Richards is working to this day. Now the picture of rich and famous, Richards "can't retire until I croak. I don't think they quite understand what I get out of this. I'm not doing it just for the money or for you. I'm doing it for me."[37]

What would you *do for yourself* if given the choice? You will have choices, and while you might choose a more traditional career path, one thing's for sure—education will not make you. History is fairly clear there. Traditional education opens some doors, but it is no guarantee of success. Hard work is the path to achievement, and that's why it's important to figure out what you're good at and what you love.

Traditional thinkers will question your pursuit of a career that requires your talent and the perhaps unconventional education that prepares you for it. But there's less and less to be said for conventional education. Jeffrey Selingo, a professor at Arizona State University, points out that while more people are going to college, "nearly half of new graduates are working jobs that don't require a bachelor's degree."[38] And Jane Shaw, a leader in the push for education reform, accuses elite universities of "doing a disservice when they lead students into majors with few, if any, job prospects."[39]

Selingo and Shaw are hardly alone in holding such views. It's a common complaint that universities aren't teaching what's relevant to the working world. That's certainly true, but it's also *always been true*. Anyone who thinks that higher education can prepare students for the work of the future assumes that education reflects what's actually happening in commerce. But it doesn't, and it can't. In a prosperous and economically dynamic society, the nature of work is always changing. Universities will always be behind the curve. So will trade schools. Even the people driving all this change can't predict the future.

In late 1977, Digital Equipment was a blue-chip technology corporation. But when its CEO, Ken Olson, was asked about the personal desktop computer that rival IBM was readying for the market, he responded that "there is no reason for any individual to have a computer in their home."[40] At the time, Harvard dropout Bill Gates's obscure startup, Microsoft, had thirty-eight employees.[41]

Gates plainly didn't agree with Olson about the future of the personal computer, and neither did his eventual rival Steve Jobs, the Reed College dropout who founded Apple Computer in 1977.[42] Four years later, Apple went public in the most oversubscribed initial public offering since 1956,[43] turning three hundred Apple employees into millionaires.

Not long after Apple went public, a pre-med student at the University of Texas named Michael Dell started PCs Limited out of his dorm room. Lacking funds to take on a lot of inventory, Dell hit on the idea of selling computers over the phone so he wouldn't have to commit capital to equipment until he had actual orders.[44]

It's a safe bet that most of those new Apple millionaires, like the tycoons at Apple's competitors, had gone to college. But had they studied computer science? It's highly unlikely. Even if their studies were related to computers in some way, what they learned in the classroom would have had little relevance to what they were doing in the *business* of computers. We know this because even the established technology companies of the era were skeptical about the future of the PC. The personal computer didn't even exist when they were in college.

Orville and Wilbur Wright were famously "first in flight." But as their biographer David McCullough notes, "they had no college education, no formal technical training, no experience working with anyone other than themselves, no friends in high places, no financial backers, no government subsidies, and little money of their own."[45] Assuming they'd had the means to attend college, what could they have been taught that would have helped them develop a flying machine?

"For years, I struggled in school," recalls the film and television producer Brian Grazer (*Splash, Parenthood, Apollo 13, Arrested Development, 24, Empire*, etc.).[46] He managed to graduate from the University of Southern California but hardly as a marquee student. So what? What school could have taught Grazer to produce a film about a man falling for a mermaid? More recently, actor-director-producer Peter Berg (*Friday Night Lights, Lone Survivor, Patriots Day*, etc.) decided, "I could probably get more following a bellman around in a hotel...for three months than I could by going to film school and learning about cameras."[47]

The Internet was introduced to consumers in the mid-1990s. It's hard to imagine a world without it today, but by the end of that decade most people around the world were still untouched by this remarkable innovation. A 1992 graduate of the University of Texas, I never took a computer course, and I didn't use email until late 1998. My experience was hardly unusual. Today, of course, just about all the work I do is Internet-related.

There are always outliers, of course, and you can find an anecdote to prove anything, including the low value of a college degree. The point, however, is that whether in entertainment, e-commerce, or any other field of business, the present rarely predicts the future. At the dawn of the twenty-first century, Britney Spears was at the top of the music world, Lance Armstrong and Tiger Woods were sports heroes *and* role models, Robert Downey Jr. and Ben Affleck were jokes in Hollywood, and the CEO of Enron was the standard by which corporate chieftains were to be judged.

Forgive the cliché, but change is the only thing that's certain. Universities talk a grand game about preparing their graduates for tomorrow, but they don't know a darned thing about tomorrow. Now, none of this is to say that you shouldn't go to college. College is great. It's a place to grow up, to be exposed to new ideas, to meet a husband or wife, and to make lifelong friends, some of whom might be crucial contacts in the working world. Moreover, a college degree is a great door-opener in the job market. That's important, especially if you're not equipped with the genius of a Steve Jobs or a Bill Gates or a Michael Dell. Even if it requires going into debt, college is generally a good idea.

My point is that what you *learn* in school will have little direct relevance to what you do when you're out. College is a way of branding yourself. A degree is a *credential* you obtain with the future in mind, but the acquired knowledge it represents is not what sets you up for success in the real world.

The United States is not the richest country in the world because it has many of the most prestigious universities in the world. The

United States has many of the world's most prestigious universities because it's the richest country in the world. Stroll around campus and note the names of great businessmen on the buildings. Our universities are an *effect* of economic growth, not the driver. To see why, let's conclude this chapter with a look at China.

In 1978, Shanghai, the commercial center of China, had only fifteen skyscrapers. By 2006, there were 3,780 of these gleaming symbols of prosperity, and the number continues to rise.[48] A visit to Shanghai or to many other cities in this rapidly growing nation reveals mind-boggling economic activity.

In the late 1970s, China was emerging from decades of doctrinaire communist rule in which property and profits were generally prohibited, and the country was predictably destitute. But with the economic liberalization that followed, China's economy took off. Today, any business that wants to grow globally has China very much in mind.

What drove this rapid transformation from poverty to prosperity? Some point to education. Writing in the *Wall Street Journal*, Paul E. Peterson and Eric A. Hamushek of the conservative Hoover Institution argue that "raising student test scores in this country up to the level in Canada would dramatically increase economic growth." Their view is that "long-run growth rates are mainly accounted for by differences in cognitive skills...."[49] The liberal *New York Times* columnist Nicholas Kristof agrees: "One reason China is likely to overtake the United States as the world's most important country in this century is that China puts more effort into building human capital than we do"[50]—an assertion that would doubtless amuse the thousands of Chinese who come to the United States each year to attend high school and college.

But these writers confuse cause and effect. If the educational thesis were true, a major factor in China's ascendance would be a top-level education system that prepared the citizenry for a sharp-elbowed capitalist world. Not so fast.

As Fox Butterfield wrote in 1982, "12 percent of those who finish primary school are unable to go on to junior high, and there is no room

in high school for 50 percent of the students who complete junior high."
Regarding access to college education, "only 3 percent of the college-age
population in China, about a million students, can get into university."[51] While most Chinese had no access to college-level instruction
in the early 1980s, 35 percent of eighteen-to-twenty-one-year-old
Americans were in college, as were 23 percent of Soviets in that age
group. Even the Philippines, whose population was a fraction of the
size of China's, could claim more college students "than in all of
China."[52]

Peterson, Hamushek, and Kristof have put the educational cart
before the production horse. It's undoubtedly true that there is a "correlation" between test scores and prosperity. But China's tremendous
economic growth began long before it was educating even a sliver of
its population. This tells us that economic freedom trumps education.
Just as America's great schools and colleges are the fruit of abundant
growth, China's growth begot good schools.

We can expect that as China's economic boom continues, top-
notch universities will follow. Rich people frequently seek status
through their kids, and sending them to exclusive schools is a popular
way of doing that. But let's not mistake cause and effect. Poorly educated for decades, the Chinese became prosperous faster than any
major nation in the history of mankind. Good schools are merely
catching up to that growth.

It's worth remembering, too, that scholars commonly predicted in
the 1980s that the superiorly educated Japanese would soon eclipse the
United States economically. And while there are many fathers of Japan's
economic slowdown since the eighties, that country's experience is a
reminder that the role of education in driving prosperity is grossly
overrated.

Just ask Jack Ma, a hapless Chinese student who failed his university entrance exams. Fortunately for him, he was turned down for every
job he applied for—even at Kentucky Fried Chicken[53]—so he founded
Alibaba, the Amazon of the Orient, and is now worth billions.

In his classic book *Wealth and Poverty*, George Gilder notes that while education and credentials are most important in government, "elsewhere most skills are learned on the job."[54] It's not that people should avoid education, but education has little to do with success in the working world.

It's said that we live in a "knowledge economy," but most people don't understand what that means. Precisely because the economy is evolving faster and faster, classroom teaching can't keep up. The "knowledge" that wins is gained by doing the work that corresponds with your skills.

We're all intelligent, but in different ways. A prosperous economy means more of us will get to express our intelligence regardless of whether an impressive degree is attached to our name.

CHAPTER FOUR

What Was Once Silly Is Now Serious

*"I can't not act. It's what I was made to do,
and I swear to God, it's the only thing I'm good at."*[1]
—Jennifer Lawrence

*"Success has a way of making the work seem less like,
well, work."*[2]
—Grant Achatz

Danny Meyer was born into a rich and prestigious St. Louis family. His maternal grandfather, Irving B. Harris, a graduate of Yale, co-founded the Toni Home Improvement Company with his brother. In 1948, they sold the business for what was then the princely sum of $20 million.[3]

Meyer's paternal grandfather, Morton Meyer, a graduate of Princeton, ran a St. Louis chemical company called Thompson-Howard. Meyer's father, Morton Louis Meyer, also a Princeton graduate, returned from service in France as an army intelligence officer to St. Louis and started a number of businesses, including a global travel services company, hotels, and restaurants.[4]

Traveling the country and the world from a young age with his father, Meyer developed an early fascination with food. He recalls a trip to Miami at the age of four on which he was "talking to anyone who would listen about the 'cwacked cwab.'" On a family trip to France when he was seven, his mother insisted that he keep a diary, in which he "chose to write about food." He liked to swap his lunch at school, "not because the other kids' lunches were better, but because this was the best way I knew of to learn about another family. I had never heard of Miracle Whip until I traded my braunschweiger on rye with another for his baloney sandwich (one slice of Oscar Mayer and Miracle Whip on Tastee white bread)."[5] By his teen years, Meyer was cooking for his friends, creatively transforming everything from hot dogs to barbecue sauce.[6]

Though he attended one of St. Louis's most prominent schools, he was an underachiever and was turned down by Princeton and Brown, eventually worming his way into Trinity College in Hartford, Connecticut.[7] He continued to work for his father's travel business during college, and his long-term plan was rather conventional.

Upon graduation, Meyer moved to New York City, not to work in travel or in restaurants, but to take a $16,500-per-year job as a special projects manager for a growing company that manufactured devices to detect shoplifters. Meyer eventually migrated to sales, where he was the company's top salesman for three straight years, earning $125,000 annually.[8]

His success led to an opportunity to open a London office for the company, but Meyer had politics on his mind. Having worked for John Anderson's quixotic 1980 presidential campaign, he thought he'd try law school. But at dinner the night before he was to take the LSAT, he admitted to an uncle, "I don't even want to be a lawyer."[9] His uncle, who had observed Meyer's lifelong fascination with food, responded, "Why don't you just do what you've been thinking about doing your whole life" and open a restaurant?[10]

Meyer took his uncle's advice. In 1984, he got a job as a daytime assistant at an Italian seafood restaurant in Manhattan, starting at the bottom—à la Keith Richards—to reach the top, with a weekly paycheck of $250.

That was quite a pay cut, but it was Meyer's first step in pursuit of his passion. As he explains, "I was born to go into business for myself—and I was destined to find a business that would allow me to share with others my enthusiasm for things I find pleasurable."[11] For Meyer, that was food. Everyone but his uncle thought he was crazy, but Meyer wasn't deterred, and in 1985 he opened Union Square Café. In what proved a wise move, the man who loved being in the kitchen fired himself as chef before the restaurant opened. Meyer would outsource the kitchen work so that he could focus his energy and intelligence on the big picture.

Union Square Café became a grand success, and Meyer was just getting started. Gramercy Tavern followed Union Square, then Eleven Madison Park, The Modern, numerous other restaurants, and a full-service catering business. Most famously, Meyer turned a hot dog cart in Madison Square Park into an international fast-casual dining concept known as Shake Shack.

In his memoir, Meyer muses about how often "people laughed at me when I said I'd be parlaying a political science degree into a career as a restaurateur!"

> [T]hey nodded politely and then winked, smiled, or gestured under the table. The common perception was that restaurants were a shady, cash-driven racket where money was always being passed illicitly and everybody kept two sets of books. This was not the career for which suburban parents sent their kids to college.[12]

But as Meyer points out, that perception of the restaurant business was dated. By the early 1980s, "many American culinary stars were being recognized and celebrated."[13] One of those stars was Wolfgang Puck. Born in Austria to a chef and a butcher, Puck left school early to work in the kitchen at Maxim's, then at the Hôtel de Paris Monte-Carlo. He came to the United States in 1973 and eventually opened

Spago on West Hollywood's then-decrepit Sunset Strip.[14] Spago's success made Los Angeles a restaurant town and was the launching pad for a global restaurant and retail operation.

When he shunned school in favor of cooking, Puck faced the same kind of skepticism Meyer experienced, but he "has seen the job of a chef change from a last-resort career to a 'rock-star profession.'" Puck tells the *Wall Street Journal*, "These days, people become cooks instead of becoming lawyers or doctors."[15] One of those people is the chef Grant Achatz, the owner of Chicago's world-renowned restaurant Alinea.

Achatz grew up in St. Clair, Michigan, "flipping eggs" at his parents' diner. The cooking bug got to him early. His friends viewed his interest in restaurants as the stuff of a "deluded dreamer," but he told himself, "I'm going to own a great restaurant, a famous one."[16]

Cooking consumed Achatz just as music had consumed Lennon and McCartney. It wasn't work to him. At culinary school, he writes, "[m]ost of the students looked at the classes as an inconvenient interruption of their leisure activities. While they were going out to bars and partying, I hit the gym every day and then spent each night reading cookbooks."[17] Food was his *education*. After scoring a job with the world-famous chef Charlie Trotter, he spent each night studying Trotter's cookbook, learning "the dishes and the techniques cold."[18]

Achatz moved on to a job at the renowned French Laundry in northern California's wine country, so thrilled by the chance to work for Thomas Keller that he didn't bother to ask what the salary was or what he would be doing. Returning to the Chicago area as head chef at Trio, he got to know Nick Kokonas, a frequent guest, and four years later the two of them opened Alinea in Lincoln Park. Within eighteen months of its opening, Alinea was ranked the number-one restaurant in the United States by *Gourmet* magazine.[19]

Achatz has since opened additional restaurants and authored the kind of cookbooks that great chefs publish. Cooking is what he loves. As he explains in his autobiography, *Life, on the Line*, "You know, it's what I do. It just makes me really happy. That's all there is to it."[20]

If Grant Achatz had been born fifty years earlier, odds are he would have labored in obscurity. While he might have loved what he was doing, the public wasn't much interested in eccentric geniuses pursuing "last resort" careers in the kitchen. Achatz is the beneficiary of a dramatic rise in prosperity that has given enough people the discretionary income and leisure to support him in the pursuit of his passion for haute cuisine. It's an economy that allowed Danny Meyer's Eleven Madison Park to hire a "coffee director" who personally prepares diners' twenty-four-dollar cups of coffee at their tables.[21]

This kind of wealth also allows individuals to concentrate on what they do best, what the nineteenth-century economist David Ricardo called "comparative advantage." Each of us does what he's good at while "importing" everything else from others. The fruits of one's labor are exchangeable for everything one needs.

Meyer recalls that before the restaurant boom he "had always noticed how many servers seemed to apologize for their work, with remarks like: 'I'm actually an actor. I'm just waiting tables until I land a real job.'"[22] If economic growth stays strong, waiters won't be embarrassed about starting off in a field that rewards creativity and flair. And those who are waiting tables on the way to becoming actors won't be smirked at either.

Several years ago, Millie, the thirteen-year-old niece of a friend in London, wrote to me:

> I have been toying with ideas for my future whilst I'm on half term and have come to the conclusion that I want to be an actress. What do you think of this idea? I think mummy thinks it's just a phase, but is beginning to realise I am serious!

Time will tell if Millie is serious about acting, but her mother's reaction was perfectly understandable. Millie's father is a successful investment banker in the city, and her parents were spending quite a lot of money to send her to one of England's top schools, with an eye on her attending a university of the Oxbridge variety. While the list of well-educated actors and actresses is long, acting has not always been viewed as a serious profession. As Lady Uckfield condescendingly asks young Simon Russell in Julian Fellowes's novel *Snobs*, "And will you always be an actor?"[23]

Apart from its want of professional cachet, acting is an extremely difficult field in which to achieve success. There are only so many roles in television, the movies, and the theater and so many people seeking them. Millie's mother's skepticism may be warranted, but it's also a bit dated. Let me explain.

The actor Roger Moore, who achieved fame in the 1960s television show *The Saint*, recalls seeing his "first TV pictures on a tiny box with a fuzzy little screen" in 1939. It was "so exciting to gather around it waiting for the valves to warm up and seeing the little picture emerge."[24] It was exciting because it was scarce. The quality of the picture, let alone the quality of the entertainment, was almost secondary.

By the 1970s, television ownership was nearly universal. Yet at the same time, there wasn't much choice for viewers, even in the United States. There were the three networks—ABC, NBC, and CBS—there was PBS, launched in 1970, and in big markets there were a few local channels that offered mostly local news, along with re-runs of shows that had previously aired on the networks. While a number of well-regarded TV programs emerged in the seventies—shows like *M*A*S*H*, *Mary Tyler Moore*, *All in the Family*, and *The Jeffersons*—television was still somewhat barren.

During that decade, Rob Lowe got into acting. His first network television show, *A New Kind of Family*, was released by ABC in 1979 in the "death slot" against ratings king *60 Minutes*. The results, Lowe writes, were predictable: "They crushed us. I mean it was a bloodletting."[25] The second episode of *A New Kind of Family* had fourteen million viewers, a sign that the series was doomed. But as Lowe points out, "today any network would kill to have our numbers. In 1979, if fourteen million people watched you, you were at death's door. Today, a huge smash like *Two and a Half Men* averages about that" number.[26] *A New Kind of Family* lasted eleven episodes.

Today, television is a completely different world. If one of the Big Three networks doesn't want you, dozens of other producers might. Compare the story of *A New Kind of Family* with that of *Mad Men*, a show that nearly died before it was born but recovered to enjoy a legendary eight-year run. Matthew Weiner labored over the pilot script for his masterpiece for seven years. HBO turned it down without so much as a phone call to say no. Luckily, the AMC cable network picked up what no one else wanted.[27]

Weiner's experience is common. *The Sopranos* is broadly viewed as one of the greatest television productions ever, but it too nearly died in the cradle. ABC, CBS, and NBC all turned it down. "Everywhere, the answer was no," writes Brett Martin in his history of the creative revolution sparked by cable television. "The universe of Dr. Melfi and Paulie Walnuts and Vesuvio and Bada Bing! seemed destined to vanish in the usual atrophic way."[28] HBO ultimately bit, however, and the rest is history. But was HBO infallible? It turns out it wasn't.

When Vince Gilligan brought *Breaking Bad* to HBO, a network known for high-quality television, they "never gave [him] an answer of any kind."[29] FX, likewise known for its critically acclaimed shows (*Nip/Tuck, Justified,* and *The Americans*, to name three), passed on it as well, opting instead for the eminently forgettable *Dirt*.[30]

The emergence of these cable networks is a result of the commoditization of television itself. With economic growth, former luxuries become everyday consumer products as entrepreneurs and businesses take what's expensive and figure out ways to make it cheap. When Roger Moore was a kid, televisions were exotic. By the time Rob Lowe began acting professionally, they were in every home, but often only one, which the whole family gathered around in the living room. Now they're everywhere.

In 2000, a fifty-inch flat-screen TV retailed for twenty thousand dollars.[31] Today, a much better fifty-inch flat screen can be purchased on Amazon.com for a little more than three hundred dollars. Most homes have one now, but is anyone watching it? Chances are you'll find each member of the family plugged into his own device—smart phone, tablet, laptop—watching his own programming on a miniature screen.

With all the screens and all the channels, producers, directors, and actors no longer have to curry favor with the three major networks. In the 2016 Emmy Awards, just about every nominee represented a show that was not a network property. The nominees for best actor in a drama, for example, were *Mr. Robot*'s Rami Malek (USA Network), Matthew Rhys from *The Americans* (FX), Liev Schreiber (*Ray Donovan*—Showtime), Bob Odenkirk (*Better Call Saul*—AMC), Kevin Spacey (*House of Cards*—Netflix), and Kyle Chandler (*Bloodline*—Netflix).

The nominees for best actress in a drama included Claire Danes (*Homeland*—Showtime), Keri Russell (*The Americans*—FX), Robin Wright (*House of Cards*—Netflix), Tatiana Maslany (*Orphan Black*—BBC America), Viola Davis (*How to Get Away with Murder*—ABC), and Taraji P. Henson (*Empire*—Fox). Of the twelve nominees in that major category, only two were from the four major networks.

Of the seven nominees for best comedy, just two were network shows—*Modern Family* and *Black-ish* (both ABC properties). It was even worse in the category of best drama. Other than PBS's *Downton Abbey*, none of the shows nominated aired on the traditional networks.[32]

We're seeing with television what we saw with restaurants: as our society becomes more affluent, stimulating the demand for what were once luxuries—like high-quality television you have to pay for—producers will emerge to meet that demand, catering to all ages and tastes. As *New York* magazine observes, "flashy TV projects roll out with almost numbing regularity now."[33] There's more to quality TV, in other words, than PBS. "Between 2009 and 2015, the number of scripted shows nearly doubled," and Netflix intends to produce six hundred hours of original television backed by $5 billion earmarked for new programs and acquisitions of others.[34]

What's even more interesting is that the Emmy nominees of 2016 didn't come only from actual television stations. Netflix, which began as an online DVD rental service, produces shows like *House of Cards*, *Bloodline*, and *Unbreakable Kimmy Schmidt* and garnered the third-most nominations. Amazon started as a book retailer in the 1990s; in 2016 it received sixteen Emmy nominations.[35] In 2013 when *House of Cards* premiered, only twenty-four original shows were streamed on the Internet. By 2017, that number had increased to 117.[36]

For actors and everyone else involved in producing this tidal wave of programming, business is booming. And the boom is not confined to Hollywood. Vancouver, a historically popular venue for TV production, is so overrun with shows that "pop-up" stages have been erected all over town to fulfill demand, and in Atlanta television producers find it hard to give crew members even a day off.[37]

What explains this revolution in entertainment? Look at your mobile phone. Back in 1989, a Tandy 5000 desktop computer—touted as the "most powerful computer ever!"—cost $8,499, monitor and mouse not included.[38] The smartphone in your pocket today would have qualified as a supercomputer then—if they could have built it, which they couldn't.

The technological advances make programs easier to consume, of course, but they also make it easier to produce, lowering the barriers to entry in the entertainment business. More directors, writers, and actors will get to pursue their passion. Millie's interest in acting becomes more plausible by the day.

Jay Leno retired from hosting NBC's *Tonight Show* in 2013. In 2016, he unveiled *Jay Leno's Garage*, a show about his love of cars and motorcycles. It began as a web-based series on NBC.com, but has since been picked up by CNBC for prime time.

Leno was always a funnyman, but he expected to be an insurance salesman like his father and assumed his comedy act would be seen only by potential clients.[39] But with the rise of comedy clubs, Leno was able to turn his passion into a career: "I watch other people and they like to go on vacation, to go out to dinner, go to athletic events. And I just write jokes. And it's seven days a week and it's fine. It's just that you have to have the stamina to do it. You just do it every day. And I like it."[40] Absolutely.

Jerry Seinfeld discovered he was funny at the age of eight. Eating milk and cookies with a friend on Long Island, Seinfeld said something so funny that the friend spit the milk and cookies back into Seinfeld's hair. He decided then and there that, "I would like to do this professionally."[41] Comedy reinforced Seinfeld's talents. Thirteen years later Seinfeld sat with his father on a bench at Eighty-first Street and Central Park West and told him that he would be going into stand-up, a declaration quite a bit more outlandish in the 1970s than Meyer's announcement that he was going into restaurants in the 1980s. But the world was changing, and Seinfeld's father seemingly knew it. He said he wished he could have gone into comedy himself.[42] Seinfeld père understood that the jobs of yesterday weren't predictors of the jobs of tomorrow. He gave his blessing.

Not everyone can be Jay Leno or Jerry Seinfeld. But those who love comedy (Boston-based Emerson College now offers a degree in "Comedic Arts"[43]) will have more opportunities to showcase their skills. The only barriers nowadays are internal. Will those who want to entertain work hard enough to make it happen? Nothing is ever easy, but it's easier to work hard if you're doing something that you love. Rob Lowe's advice to young actors is "Say yes to *any* opportunity to grow and/or do good work. You never know where it will lead or who may be paying attention."[44] The possibility of being discovered grows by the day. Acting and entertaining are very serious for those who can't imagine doing anything else.

CHAPTER FIVE

Abundant Profits Make Possible the Work That Isn't

"[P]eople give away more money when
they have more money."[1]
—James Q. Wilson

I n 1997, Roberto C. Goizueta died after a battle with lung cancer. The front-page story about him in the *Wall Street Journal* noted that the legendary CEO of the Coca-Cola Company had little interest in "high-profile civic involvement" in his adopted city of Atlanta, Georgia, but "thanks to his 16 years of focusing strictly on business, many a civic cause here is better off."[2]

For Goizueta, his every work day was all about attaining profits for the owners of Coca-Cola. He delivered. Coke was valued at $4 billion when he took over as CEO in 1981. Its market capitalization had reached $145 billion by the time he died in 1997.[3]

The surge in the value of Coca-Cola has had an enormous effect on Atlanta, where the company is based. Bill Warren, a pediatrician, inherited Coke shares, and the rise in their value gave him the means to close his medical practice in the suburbs and volunteer at an inner-city health clinic serving the poor.

Thanks to a gift of Coke stock, Emory University's endowment grew from $250 million in 1981 to $3.8 billion the year of Goizueta's death. The *Wall Street Journal* observed, "Finding a building on the Emory campus that doesn't bear the name of a Coke figure is a trick: Locals half-jokingly refer to the school as Coca-Cola U," and added, "Emory has built facilities, boosted research, offered scholarships and endowed professorships and expanded programs" largely because of an endowment massively expanded by the success of one company.[4]

In 1980, the Atlanta-based Robert W. Woodruff, Joseph P. White-head, Lettie Pate Evans, and Lettie Pate Whitehead foundations gave less than $5 million to Atlanta causes. In 1997, the four donated roughly $220 million. Among their beneficiaries were the Fernbank Museum of Natural History ($10 million to help it pay down debt) and Centennial Olympic Park, a principle venue of the 1996 Atlanta Olympic Games. Agnes Scott College, a liberal arts institution in Atlanta, saw its endowment grow from $34 million in 1981 to $425 million. As the school's president acknowledged, "Coca-Cola stock has kept this college alive during difficult times and now makes it thrive."[5]

The story of Coca-Cola's success and its impressive implications for Atlanta's charitable institutions is a reminder that profits make it possible for many needy students to attend college, for others to attain medical care that otherwise would be too costly, and for quite a few others to choose work that has nothing to do with profit-making. And all the billions that have gone to charity because of the soft-drink maker's success will pale in comparison to the giving of the future.

Indeed, as *Fortune* magazine reported in 2010, "Bill Gates, Melinda Gates and Warren Buffett are asking the nation's billionaires to pledge at least half their net worth to charity, in their lifetime or at death." Gates—the world's second richest man—told *Fortune* that 50 percent of one's wealth is a "low bar" for giving, while Buffett—not far behind—has pledged to give away 99 percent of his wealth.[6]

Buffett has been a major donor to the Bill & Melinda Gates Foundation, which has pursued such lofty goals as eradicating global poverty and disease and empowering women to transform their lives. You can do that when wealth is abundant. The Gates Foundation employs 1,376 persons in its efforts to make the world a better place with an endowment of some $39 billion.[7] And in time, the Gates Foundation will be dwarfed by other, bigger foundations.

Indeed, in December 2015, Mark Zuckerberg, the founder of Facebook, and his wife, Priscilla Chan, pledged to give away 99 percent of their Facebook stock to charity. Chan Zuckerberg Science, an offshoot of the Chan Zuckerberg Initiative, LLC, already has $3 billion behind it and employs, the *Wall Street Journal* reports, "dozens of top scientists who think it is possible to cure, prevent or manage diseases by the end of the century."[8] It's not crazy to speculate that Zuckerberg's grandchildren might be born into a world no longer ravaged by cancer thanks to the generosity of their grandparents. When Zuckerberg and Chan made that pledge, it amounted to more than $45 billion,[9] but if Facebook continues to grow as many investors expect, the gift could be many multiples of that.

If you're interested in a life of nonprofit work, you should consider what charitable giving will look like thirty years from now. I contend that the global economy will continue to grow. If so, it's likely that the charitable donations of Buffett, Gates, and Zuckerberg will look small compared with future bequests. I base that prediction on the popular annual report on great wealth, the *Forbes* 400, a listing of America's richest that began in 1982. In 2014, only thirty-four names from the original list were still among the four hundred richest Americans. While a net worth of $75 million got you into the *Forbes* 400 in 1982, the price of entry was $1.5 billion by 2014.[10]

With the exception of a few mild recessions and the big one in 2008, the U.S. economy has grown fairly rapidly since 1982, and the ranks of the richest have changed constantly. Mark Zuckerberg was a high school student in 2000, but by 2015 he was pledging to give away tens of billions.

If the U.S. and world economies continue to grow, the richest people in the world in 2046 will be a very different crowd from those of today. And the wealth in the hands of the superrich thirty years from now promises to be mind-boggling.

It's safe to say that many more billions—and probably trillions—of dollars, will be in the hands of foundations eager to fix what's wrong with the world, making the employment possibilities for those who want to join that idealistic work promising indeed. But never forget that nonprofit institutions are an *effect* of broad prosperity achieved in the private sector.

In short, for those who desire a fulfilling life of nonprofit work, extraordinary wealth creation is your best friend. The more wealth that's produced and the more profits that are made, the more that will be available for the good works of the nonprofits.

In the mid-2000s, Arthur C. Brooks, then a professor at Syracuse University, studied charitable giving and was astounded by what he found. For one thing, Americans are big givers. Three out of four U.S. families give to charity each year, and their giving works out to roughly 3.5 percent of their income. And since the United States is a rich country, that 3.5 percent amounts to a lot of charitable giving each year. "Private American giving could more than finance the entire annual gross domestic product (GDP) of Sweden, Norway, or Denmark," he writes.[11]

Brooks finds that Americans are steady givers: "Charitable contributions in the United States over the past fifty years have always been between 1.5 and 2 percent of GDP."[12] And only 20 percent of American donors give with a tax deduction in mind.[13] There is much generosity in this country. Americans plainly enjoy creating wealth, but they also enjoy helping others and advancing the arts, education, and policy with their money.

As you would assume, given the extraordinary charitable contributions of people like Buffett, Gates, and Zuckerberg, the rich account for a big portion of total donations. Brooks found that the U.S. households in the top 10 percent of income accounted for at least a quarter of all the money donated, while households with a net worth of more than one million dollars (about 7 percent of the U.S. population) were the source of half of all charitable gifts.[14] It helps to have a booming stock market. Brooks tracked giving from 1995 to 2000, when stocks were soaring, and found that "household giving exploded by 54 percent."[15]

The pattern is fairly clear. Economic growth begets wealth creation, which begets lots of charitable giving. The countless nonprofit organizations in the United States are the fruit of our wealth. And while the average American gives away five and a half times what the average German donates,[16] it's not unreasonable to suppose that as the rest of the world starts to catch up with American wealth creation, the global nonprofit sector will boom, and with it, work opportunities for those who choose this path.

To see up close how this works, let's turn to the memoirs of Blair Tindall, the author of *Mozart in the Jungle*, an account of her life as an oboe player in New York. You may know that title from the Emmy-winning Amazon television show loosely based on Tindall's book.

Mozart in the Jungle is a reminder that without wealth creation, there would be no high culture. That makes wealth creation important for people like Tindall, who writes, "I would trade almost anything to play the oboe."[17] Because this is a rich country, she's able to do that.

To see how classical music developed in the United States, it's best to begin in 1908, when the tycoons Andrew Carnegie (steel), J. P. Morgan (finance), and Joseph Pulitzer (newspapers) donated ninety thousand dollars to the New York Philharmonic. Pulitzer also bequeathed ten times that amount to the orchestra at his death.[18]

Relying heavily on the generosity of the rich, the arts suffer when wealth creation stumbles. U.S. donations to the arts fell from $1.4 million in 1930 to $740,000 in 1933, during the Great Depression.[19] Likewise, the arts do well when the rich do well (and get to hold onto their money). It cost $185 million to build New York's Lincoln Center in the 1950s and 60s, and $144 million of that came from private sources with names like Ford, Rockefeller, and Carnegie. When Lincoln Center nearly went bankrupt in its seventh year, John D. Rockefeller III and Lawrence Wien donated $1.25 million each to keep it afloat.[20]

While symphonies across the country raised $30 million in 1970, by 1990 that figure had increased to $290 million.[21] The U.S. economy recessed a bit in the early 1990s, and the situation for orchestras and symphonies looked dire. But then a technology boom bailed out these persistently unprofitable institutions. As Tindall reports, "In 1995 alone, the average endowment increased among the nation's fifty largest orchestras by 76 percent." As the stock market rose, so did endowments.

The effect of rising endowments is probably pretty easy for readers to predict at this point. Flush with private wealth, orchestras could pay more. By 2003, Tindall writes that "at least seven orchestras paid their music directors more than $1 million, with two earning over $2 million. Ten paid their executives over $300,000, with three paying more than $700,000. Player pay, which steadily averages around 43 percent of an orchestra's budget, saw raises of 3.2 to 5 percent between 1994 and 1999."[22] This is where it gets interesting.

In the early 1960s, Tindall writes, "Symphony players worked day jobs to survive, since their orchestras played only partial seasons."[23] But the fortunes of classical musicians soon began to change. In 1964, the New York Philharmonic began paying its musicians full-time salaries of ten thousand dollars per year. In 1966, the Ford Foundation gave $80 million in matching grants to establish endowments for sixty-one orchestras. "Seemingly overnight, classical musicians could view an orchestra job as full-time employment, complete with health and pension benefits and paid time off for illness and vacation."[24]

Tindall herself embarked on her musical career in the 1970s, and the trend of full-time work continued. Rich people, who seem to derive great satisfaction from contributing to the arts, fueled a building boom in arts centers, which had to be filled with musicians—musicians who now could expect full-time pay for pursuing their passion.

By the 1980s, the Cincinnati Symphony Orchestra had a budget of $31 million that made it possible for its one hundred musicians to earn a minimum of $85,000 per year with nine weeks of paid vacation.[25] In 2003, the base pay at the New York Philharmonic was $103,000, and many musicians earned quite a bit more. And while musicians outside of New York didn't earn as much, living expenses were lower. Minimum pay at the Baltimore Symphony Orchestra was $73,000, $56,000 in Milwaukee, and $27,000 in Charlotte.[26] Musicians weren't necessarily getting rich, but they were earning a living doing what it would pain them *not* to do.

This story is all the more remarkable because it involves a business—classical music—that "is clearly failing," as Tindall admits.[27] A symphony orchestra is the epitome of a *nonprofit* business. If not for their donors, they would disappear in most cities, perhaps even New York. Great wealth benefits us all. Just ask your local oboist.

Or university president. Some people think that big-time college sports is a disgrace to American academia. But let's look at it more closely. The University of Alabama's head football coach, Nick Saban, earns more than $11 million annually. Only $200,000 of that is paid by the university; the rest is a "talent fee" paid to Saban by the booster-funded Crimson Tide Foundation.[28] That's a lot of money in a state with a median income of $43,000, but there's a case to be made that Saban is vastly *underpaid*, and not just because he's arguably the greatest college football coach ever to walk the field.

Consider Saban's impact on the University of Alabama. When he arrived in Tuscaloosa in 2007, the university was completing a $50 million capital campaign for its athletic department. With Saban aboard, the campaign concluded with more than twice that amount. The athletic department budget was $68 million per year in 2007. By 2014, it was $153 million, $95 million of that directly related to the football program.[29]

The former University of Alabama president Robert Witt told *60 Minutes* that Saban was the "best financial investment this university

has ever made." And Witt wasn't talking only about the athletic department. The Crimson Tide's gridiron success contributed to the success
of a university-wide $500 million capital campaign. Enrollment? It's
increased by fourteen thousand students since 2007. Before Saban,
Alabama accepted 77 percent of its applicants. Nowadays, its admit-
tance rate is a little more than 50 percent.[30]

Ohio State's head football coach, Urban Meyer, earns $6.5 million
annually. But as of the opening of the 2015 football season, the athletic
department's revenues had increased 14 percent to $69 million, while
merchandise sales had risen $3 million. Michigan's Jim Harbaugh has
a salary of $9 million. But after his arrival, the school had to put a halt
on season ticket sales, so high was the demand, and the Wolverine
athletic department signed a $169 million deal with Nike.[31] Pre-Har-
baugh, Michigan's football fortunes were very much in decline. But if
he proves as good at Michigan as he was at Stanford and for the 49ers
of the NFL, it's only a matter of time before donations to the University
of Michigan increase enormously.

Each of these universities fields a variety of teams that don't earn
a profit. Football pays the bills for many sports, enabling countless
student-athletes to pursue their passion. And as the numbers from
Alabama show, a successful football team stimulates contributions to
the university as a whole and improves the quality of students matriculating. Profits truly make it possible for many more of us to do what
we enjoy. Nowhere is that more evident than in the city in which I live,
Washington, D.C.

I moved here in 2003 to work as a fundraiser for the libertarian
Cato Institute. It was a way to pay the bills so that I could write about
economic policy in my free time. I still work part-time in fundraising,
now for FreedomWorks. Both of these organizations are funded
entirely by private donations, mostly from well-to-do individuals. Each
year they hold retreats for their donors, at which their scholars invariably begin their presentations by thanking the donors. With good
reason. Because of their extraordinary generosity, there are no dreary

Sundays and bluesy Mondays for Cato or FreedomWorks scholars, who get to pursue the kind of work that they love.

Cato and FreedomWorks and the hundreds of other policy institutions, covering every issue under the sun, are the fruit of abundant prosperity outside of Washington. To appreciate them, visit a country like Peru, Haiti, or Bangladesh, where the nonprofits are funded by outsiders, including generous Americans. In 2002 alone, private sources in the United States gave $50 billion to international causes.[32]

Inside the United States, nonprofit policy organizations full of talented and passionate people are ubiquitous because Americans are both rich and generous. Profits make nonprofit work possible.

Profits and wealth are compassionate. We know this from anecdotes about Buffett, Gates, and Zuckerberg, but we also know this empirically. Charitable contributions in the United States grow as the economy grows. There's a clear relationship. We can see it with our own eyes. In 2015, HBO released a short but uplifting documentary, *Open Your Eyes*, that powerfully demonstrated this correlation.

Cataracts have blinded countless people around the world. Happily, technological advances enable doctors to remove cataracts and implant intraocular lenses, restoring sight to those who had lost it. That technology, however, hasn't reached the poorest parts of the world, where many are needlessly blind.

Intraocular lens implants used to cost five hundred dollars per eye, but now they cost as little as two dollars. *Open Your Eyes* shows the impoverished elderly of Nepal getting a chance to see again from doctors who devote one day a week to treating them at no charge. In a world without profits, the blind would never get to see again. As Arthur Brooks explains, "Without prosperity, large-scale charity is impossible."[33] And without prosperity, those who wanted to do that compassionate work wouldn't have a chance.

The 2016 Paralympics, held in financially distressed Brazil, suffered serious cutbacks because the host country couldn't afford the necessary workers and facilities.[34] This is what slow growth gets us. But when the profit motive is encouraged, what used to be costly and obscure becomes cheap and common.

Profits and prosperity allow us to be compassionate.

CHAPTER SIX

The Millennial Generation Will Be the Richest Yet—
Until the Next One

"Do you ever get tired of making love?"[1]
—Tony Bennett, when asked if he ever gets tired of
singing "I Left My Heart in San Francisco"

The 1994 cult hit *Reality Bites* follows Lelaina (Winona Ryder), Troy (Ethan Hawke), and Vickie (Janeane Garofalo) as they navigate post-collegiate life in Houston. It's not a great movie, but it reflects the struggles of twenty-somethings in the early 1990s, when economic growth was weak. Lelaina is an underemployed office worker with designs on a career as a documentary filmmaker, the musically passionate Troy is perpetually unemployed, and Vickie is folding shirts at the Gap.

Reality Bites wasn't the first film of its kind. *Slacker* (1991), a mock documentary, follows overeducated but underemployed misfits in Austin, Texas, and *Singles* (1992) chronicles the doings of six single characters in their twenties in grunge-era Seattle—a far cry from the booming Seattle of today.

This seemingly aimless generation inspired a book too. Douglas Coupland's *Generation X: Tales for an Accelerated Culture* (1991) profiles Andy, Claire, and Dag, who have recently quit "pointless jobs done grudgingly to little applause." Like their overeducated counterparts in

Reality Bites, Slacker, and *Singles,* they've graduated into "low-pay, low-prestige, low-benefit, no-future jobs in the service industry."

Many college graduates of the early nineties grimly believed they were entering a world of limited opportunity. Unlike their fortunate upper-middle-class parents, the members of Generation X faced a future of unfulfilling work and declining standards of living. Does any of this sound familiar?

Then the downcast mood of Generation X was suddenly dissipated. On August 9, 1995, Netscape, with its famous web browser, was taken public in a monster IPO, changing everything. A generation that was supposedly doomed to poorly paid service work and living in crowded and grungy share houses found its way.

While most Americans in 1995 knew little about computers and the Internet, recent college graduates had a fairly advanced understanding. They were familiar with personal computers and the technology that animated their primitive (by today's standards) features. If computers and the Internet were the future of commerce, Generation X would write the story. And so it did.

Yahoo went public in 1996, Amazon in 1997, and eBay in 1998. Capital frantically poured into California's Silicon Valley in pursuit of the next great Internet start-up, and Generation X, outfitted with the requisite technological know-how, benefited handsomely from the economic transformation.

So powerful was technology's lure that even the blue-chip investment bank Goldman Sachs suffered a talent drain, its "Gen X" employees giving up generous pay and perks in favor of stock options potentially worth millions. The generation that was going to have to get used to lower living standards than Mom and Dad enjoyed was soon the richest generation yet. This is a story that today's downcast Millennials need to keep in mind as all the pundits the media can serve up tell them, "Learn to do without."

Robert Samuelson wrote in the *Washington Post* back in 2011, "A specter haunts America: downward mobility. Every generation, we believe, should live better than its predecessors," but "[f]or young Americans, the future could be dimmer."[2] And in 2014 *National Review*'s Kevin Williamson issued a warning for "Generation Vexed": "They may communicate with smiley faces and 140-character bursts of text, but Millennials still have sufficient command of the English language to comprehend the fact that they're getting, in the words of an earlier and happier and more fortunate generation, *hosed*."[3]

The economic future of today's young people might look bleak at first glance, especially after the weakness of the recovery following the financial crisis of 2008. But laments that life will never be as good as it was in the past are nothing new. Steven Hayward showed in *The Age of Reagan* that fears about the economic fortunes of American youth tend to correlate with periods of weak economic growth. When, amid the stagflation of the late 1970s, President Jimmy Carter's pollster found that "a majority of Americans thought that their children's lives would be worse than their own,"[4] the president himself joined the mourners: "I think it's inevitable that there will be a lower standard of living than what everybody had always anticipated...." He concluded that the "only trend is downward. But it's been almost impossible to get people to face up to this."[5]

The philosopher Eric Hoffer had observed a few years earlier that America's young "are not willing to do the hard work by which alone the world can be improved. Hearing what they say, and seeing what they do, one suspects that one of the main functions of the young's idealism is finding good reasons for doing bad things. One has the impression that [the] young do not want to, or perhaps cannot, grow up."[6]

But then the 1980s happened. The generation that was supposed to accept a lower standard of living than their parents enjoyed produced what some called the "Decade of Greed." To this day, the enduring symbol of the 1980s is the "young, upwardly mobile professional"— the "yuppie." The children who were supposed to do without became the generation that had everything.

The economic gloom hanging over the Millennial generation is evidence that there is no new thing under the sun. Mark my words: the Millennials will wind up the richest generation in the history of the richest nation in the history of the world.

This will be true because of economic fundamentals that the pundits too often ignore. We produce so that we can consume. More to the point, to produce is to transact. In any economy, wealth is created through the exchange of the goods or services that one person has produced for the goods or services produced by someone else. Each generation eclipses the previous one because technology is continuously lowering the barriers to transactions.

Two centuries ago, markets expanded with steamships and trains. Then came the automobile, which dramatically expanded the markets that entrepreneurs could serve. Then came the airplane, then the personal computer. Most recently, the Internet has annihilated distance in transactions (think Amazon.com), massively increasing the number of people who can produce and transact with others.

The expansion of markets through technology is making the rapid accumulation of enormous wealth easier. WhatsApp had a mere fifty-five employees when Facebook acquired it for $19 billion. Uber, whose physical product is nothing more than an "app" that connects drivers and passengers, is now valued in the neighborhood of $60 billion. YouTube, with a workforce that numbered in the teens, commanded more than a billion dollars from Google in 2006.

Millennials—the generation that communicates "with smiley faces and 140-character bursts of text"—are the generation most attuned to the capabilities of this new technology. Having grown up with it, they understand how it's evolving and appreciate the staggering commercial possibilities it is opening up. While Generation X made millions on the Internet back in the 1990s, exponentially greater global connectivity allows today's twenty-somethings to pursue *billions.*

In 2015, Silicon Valley was home to 124 "unicorns,"[7]—relatively young start-ups valued at more than a billion dollars. Will all of them survive? Of course not. Neither did most of the Valley companies from the 1990s. And that's the point. Silicon Valley isn't the richest region in the world because all of its companies succeed. It's the richest precisely because many of its start-ups fail. Success is about information, which is embodied in the wins and losses in technology.

But Millennials' success won't be the product of technology alone. As we've seen, prosperity drives up the consumption of a huge range of goods and services. In the years ahead, as substantially greater wealth chases more goods and services, the variety of jobs producing those goods and services will explode.

Naysayers write off the Millennials as the most coddled, spoiled, and entitled generation in history, but the older you are, the more easily you should see through such complaints. *Every* new generation is coddled, spoiled, and entitled, and the reason is what we call *progress*. Thanks to economic growth, today's youth expect a lot from their employers, and given their potential productivity, their expectations are reasonable. And if they're spoiled and entitled, that's because amazing economic advances have allowed each generation to grow up with more than the one before it. Millennials appear spoiled because they grew up free from great hardship.

Fortunately, their entitled ways will not keep them from producing. Since everyone wants more, Millennials will produce in order to get more—and that's exactly what markets are signaling. *USA Today* reported in 2016, "Every major hotel company has designed a new brand to appeal to these consumers in their 20s and early 30s whose purchasing power and desire to travel is suspected to increase exponentially in the coming years."[8] Hoteliers aren't launching new brands to fulfill the needs of slackers living in their parents' basements. We can read the same market signals on Wall Street. Investment firms, which make money by attracting the savings of earners, are busy courting Millennials.[9]

Wait and see: the generation that supposedly doesn't know how to work will be the richest generation yet.

CHAPTER SEVEN

My Story

*"I have never believed in myself more than when I was
writing my script. I was never happier with myself."*[1]
—Dominick Dunne, *The Way We Lived Then*

"How do you like school?" Yogi Berra replied, "Closed."[2]

I'm going to pause now to share the story of my own career, not
because it's extraordinary but because it's in fact pretty ordinary.
My story illustrates how economic evolution has expanded the
range of work options. When I graduated from college in 1992, there
was no Internet to speak of. Within a few years, as I'll explain, it made
my career as a writer possible.

My story is also a reminder that the path to the job that aligns with
your talents and passion is often rocky and marked by failures. I don't
mind saying that fear propelled me much of the time.

After years of moving around as my dad wrapped up his time in
the U.S. Navy and attended business school, my parents moved my
sister and me to Pasadena, California, in 1975. From kindergarten
through the third grade I attended Linda Vista School, which was right
in the neighborhood.

Our classroom bookshelves contained the "Meet" series of biographies of great Americans—*Meet George Washington, Meet Abraham Lincoln, Meet Martin Luther King,* and many others. My favorite was *Meet Thomas Jefferson.* I couldn't get enough of the "Meet" books, and that seemed to be a problem.

Though I was in the middle of every game at recess, in the classroom I kept to myself, poring over those short books. Because of my consuming interest in those biographies, my parents and relatives bought me more and more books about historical figures, especially U.S. presidents.

Still, by second grade I found it hard to pay attention in class, and one night I told my parents that school wasn't going well because I was reading all the time instead of following what was going on in class. My parents were relieved when my teacher told them she was pleased with my love of reading. As long as I kept my nose in books, she said, everything would be fine.

I liked history and writing, tolerated math, and loathed science. Sports made attending school fun, but probably like most kids I dreaded Sunday nights.

In high school, the math became much more difficult. Freshman geometry went way over my head, and Algebra II as a sophomore merely added to my angst. It was doable, but there was nothing fun or interesting about it. It was assumed that these classes were essential if you were college-bound, and I got by with Bs and the occasional C.

As a junior I transferred to Loyola High School, west of downtown Los Angeles. Unfortunately, my extreme dislike of math in no way subsided. An advanced algebra class was beyond my capabilities—or at least beyond my willingness to work hard—so I dropped it. One of the counselors warned me this would be difficult to explain to colleges. It was all so depressing.

My grades reflected my middling interest in school. I wasn't one to act up, but the only classes that captivated me were history and literature. Cs in math and science kept my grade point average in check. Nevertheless, I remained a voracious reader.

The first hardcover book I ever bought was *Mafia Princess* by Antoinette Giancana, a purchase motivated by my fascination with the mob. The entertainment industry also captivated me, and I read a history of *Saturday Night Live*, a biography of Frank Sinatra, and the story of a 1970s financial scandal inside Columbia Pictures, *Indecent Exposure*. Business reads included Lee Iacocca's autobiography and Ken Auletta's *Greed and Glory on Wall Street* (about the original fall of Lehman Brothers in the 1980s). Herman Wouk's *The Winds of War* and *War and Remembrance* had me entranced in the months it took me to read both, and I was an early fan of James Webb (the future senator), whose novels dealt with life at the Naval Academy, combat in Vietnam, and military life in general. After nights out drinking with friends, I'd come home to read books.

My grades reflected my boredom in school, and I overheard my disappointed father telling friends that his son had "priced himself out of" top colleges. It was true.

In a senior-year class on public policy, our textbook was *Newsweek* magazine. I couldn't believe my luck. This wasn't work because it was too much fun to be work. I'd been reading for years about current events, so I was way ahead. Needless to say, I was the top student in that class, and I always had my hand up. For the first time in many years, I was the teacher's pet. My A-plus in that class was another signal about my talents.

To my high school counselor's surprise, I was admitted to Cornell University, but I wanted a college with big-time football, so I chose the University of Texas. It was just my luck that the Longhorns endured three losing seasons during my four years in Austin.

I majored in government and did B-minus work. My problem was having too much free time, but a part-time job during my senior year finally forced me to use my time more wisely, and my grades went up. But that's really not the point.

Even though I slept through lots of classes, I was interested in learning. I read the *Wall Street Journal* cover to cover, with special interest in the editorial page, as well as policy-focused books by economists such as Walter Williams and Thomas Sowell. And then I spent a lot of time in the UT library reading back issues of countless magazines covering everything from entertainment (*Vanity Fair*) to sports (*Sporting News*) to current events (*National Review*). Fiction and nonfiction books were all around me.

Sophomore year, I ran for student body president—mostly for fun, as I didn't expect to win—but the enjoyment I got out of talking policy publicly was yet another signal of what most interested me. All this became more apparent when I spent a semester abroad during my junior year.

The program I signed up for was Semester at Sea, which is able to offer generous financial aid because of its benefactors. Students travel the world on a ship, taking classes while at sea and visiting countries such as India, China, Brazil, Venezuela, Cuba, Kenya, and South Africa. Semester at Sea was the best thing I did in college, and I easily learned the most from it. One of my professors on the ship was Richard Lamm, the former governor of Colorado. I loved his class on public policy, and once again I was the top student.

By my senior year, it should have been obvious that I ought to look for work in public policy, but I didn't see it that way. As far as I could tell, I had no obvious path. Paid jobs in Washington were scarce, and moving there to work for nothing or next to nothing didn't make sense to me or my parents. In the spring of 1992, I thought the possibility of work that interested me was slim.

I interviewed at investment banks, but this was a slow period for the economy, and they weren't interested in seniors with 2.7 GPAs. Eventually I got a job with NDE Environmental, a struggling technology company based in Los Angeles. I moved to Houston and was assigned a sales role in Texas and Louisiana. NDE tested underground gasoline storage tanks for leaks, and my job was to sell our services and oversee several technicians.

It was a great experience in many ways. I found sales difficult but also reinforcing and somewhat remunerative as I built the business from nothing into something that was profitable. My confidence as a salesman grew.

At the same time, since I didn't understand the technology, I was a disaster as a manager. Fortunately, I was so successful at building the business that I was sent to Chicago to start all over again, building up our business throughout the Midwest. Still, when the technicians called me in the middle of the night with questions, I rarely had answers. I didn't know what they did and was too lazy to learn. My ignorance made me a poor manager and kept me from being able to talk to my customers' engineers.

After successfully building the Midwest business, I was promoted to national sales manager at the company's new headquarters in Austin. I still didn't understand the technology, but I planned to go back to school for an MBA after my fourth year with NDE. Mediocre college grades and a conventional résumé kept me out of the top-tier business schools, but I made it into the perfectly respectable Owen Graduate School of Management at Vanderbilt.

Given my aversion to numbers, business school might seem like an odd choice, but that's what people did then, and still do. For good or for ill, it's fairly simple to hide your weaknesses at business school because so much of the work is group-focused.

I was pretty hopeless in the finance and accounting classes, but the school's aversion to failing students meant that I got through them with low Cs. Other classes involved group work, so I would usually write up the reports while others handled the numbers. I was fine in the economics classes because I was interested in the subject. Many of the classes involved presenting ideas, and this was tailor-made for me. After all, I was still an avid reader who also liked speaking.

Despite average grades in my first year, I received an offer of an internship with Goldman Sachs, then as now very much *the* investment bank. There was a bull market in 1997, and Goldman was eagerly staffing up its private client services (PCS) group to gather the rising assets of America's super rich. This work didn't require arcane financial expertise as much as sales skills.

The summer internship at Goldman was posh. Lots of fancy dinners but minimal work. It didn't seem to matter that I was not a numbers guy. If you were at Goldman, it was assumed you were fairly bright, and an intern's work didn't stretch the brain too much.

There was one scary exercise that would take place at random intervals. The intern coordinator, Bobby Zrike, would out of nowhere call "open meetings," at which summer associates had to answer questions. Fortunately for me, most of the questions pertained to the stock market and current events, allowing me to shine. I came off as smart and personable and had a successful internship. At the end of business school, I came to New York PCS. It was 1999, and the bull market was still raging. It was seemingly a great time to build a PCS business, particularly at Goldman Sachs, whose private client division covered nearly half of the *Forbes* 400.

I wrote good prospecting letters and was able to get meetings with a lot of rich people, but I ignored the advice from management to find an existing team to work with. That was the direction that Goldman PCS was heading in, and it would have benefited someone like me, who lacked quantitative skills. Why not join a team so that I could focus on getting prospects in the door while more numerate but shyer team members formulated asset-allocation pitches? Comparative advantage works in all walks of life.

Instead, I foolishly went it alone, expecting people to entrust the fruits of their life's work to a kid in his twenties with no real financial and market knowledge. I was good at getting meetings but had little interest in the actual Goldman products. Rather, I remained interested in policy. My favorite part of the week was Friday afternoon after the markets had closed—not because the weekend was ahead, but because I'd watch my hero Larry Kudlow debate inflation with Bill Wolman and the *Wall Street Journal*'s Jacob Schlesinger on CNBC.

It was then that I started doing something that Goldman man-agement would have frowned on if they had known about it but that set the stage for my future work. In the late 1990s and early 2000s, economic pundits were talking about inflation, and with the excep-tion of Kudlow, just about all of them regarded inflation as the result of too much economic growth and too many people working. I was in disbelief.

Having grown up in the 1970s, I knew that inflation revealed itself when growth was slow to nonexistent. Inflation is a devaluation of the currency. Currency devaluation invariably leads to slower growth because the investors whose capital fuels new businesses and jobs become more cautious. Why invest if future returns will come back in devalued money? Excited by seeing what the economics establishment was missing, I began writing commentaries about inflation for my small client base. Suddenly, I was having a lot of fun.

But it wasn't my job to be an amateur economic commentator for Goldman's clients. I knew what my real job was, and I would look around the floor and see people who truly loved the aspects of the job that I couldn't stand. While spreadsheets and price-to-earnings ratios terrified me, they animated my colleagues. I was self-aware enough then to realize that this job made no sense for me. Although I enjoyed pursuing clients, I had little interest in the day-to-day work of tailoring Goldman's amazing collection of products to the financial needs of potential clients.

Stocks hit record highs in March 2000 and then began a long descent. At least I had so few clients that I didn't have to handle many of the calls wondering why I or Goldman had lost them so much money.

Around this time, I was having—you guessed it—a serious policy discussion with a Goldman colleague. My focus was always elsewhere, but in this argument about who-knows-what, this Goldman veteran snapped me into reality: if stocks continued to decline, there would be mass layoffs in the firm. Until that point, I had never considered the possibility of being made redundant. Yet the conversation that day was the wake-up call that I needed. The Internet and technology boom that had made my employment at Goldman possible was in correction mode in a big way. Not long afterwards, a company-wide voicemail from Goldman's chairman, Henry Paulson, (email wasn't as widely used in the early 2000s) indicated that layoffs were likely.

I somehow made it to 2001, but by the spring layoffs had begun, and I was told that my job was in jeopardy. I was terrified, but that was good. I finally reached out to a Goldman veteran about teaming up, and his broad knowledge of the markets combined with my skill at getting meetings brought a few name clients through the door. I thought I might survive, but meetings with management indicated that my employment was still in serious trouble. It was agony, and I found myself hoping to contract some kind of major illness as a way of avoiding the inevitable.

The inevitable became devastatingly real on the Thursday before Memorial Day weekend in 2001. To Goldman's credit, they didn't require the laid off (there were many) to clean off their desks in public but had administrative staff box up our possessions and send them to us.

One of the hardest calls I've ever made was the one to my father. My mother called me the next day and sobbed uncontrollably. My agony was hers. I didn't want to be out in public because I didn't want to explain my situation to friends. But they knew too. And although job loss is often healthy, both for the person and the economy, it can still be devastating for the individual, not to mention the managers who must deliver the bad news.

Painful as they are, recessions serve an important purpose. During booms a lot of workers find their way into the wrong jobs and a lot of mistaken investments take place. The correction of mis-hires and faulty investments are part of economic growth, paradoxical as that may sound. Failure is information, for the laid-off worker and for the investor. Indeed, the economy wouldn't grow if we didn't have failure. Still, my own unemployment was hard to take at the time.

Luckily for me, Goldman Sachs is a great company to leave. It's so highly regarded that its former employees are viewed as attractive hires. In denial, I followed some former colleagues to Credit Suisse PCS. Eager to correct my past mistakes, I joined a top team right away. I was one of the lucky ones, if spending another year in the wrong business was lucky. I was so eager to be on a team that I didn't search for a good fit. While I could still get good meetings, I was with the wrong people. I didn't trust them, and as the post-9/11 stock market was still weak, it wasn't a great time to be hunting for new clients.

It may have been a terrible year at Credit Suisse, but my interest in policy writing remained strong. Assigned a few clients upon arrival at Credit Suisse, I was writing economic commentary for them. One client perceptively pointed out to me that I was in the wrong job. At about the same time, I made contact with the economist Arthur Laffer, who put me in touch with one of the economists on his staff, who told me to buy his book on monetary policy. It fascinated me. Noticing that he'd written it while at H. C. Wainwright Economics in Boston and suspecting that my time at Credit Suisse wouldn't end well, I sent a letter to Wainwright's president, David Ranson, to ask about a job—a job I was actually interested in doing.

In September 2002 I moved to Boston to work for Wainwright, selling their empirical economic research to fund managers who used it to allocate capital. "Empirical" meant *numbers*, but I understood where Ranson was coming from. Finally, I was selling something I understood (for the most part). Even better, Ranson allowed me to write reports on the economy. Four years after graduating from business school, I was actually doing something I enjoyed. And I was getting to write for clients out in the open. As painful as losing my job had been, it finally forced me down a new path—the *right* path for me. If Goldman had kept me on, I might have more money, but I'd have a lot less confidence.

Ranson taught me an enormous amount, but the market was still weak and many of Wainwright's clients were leaving. Convinced that I was in the path of another downsizing, I started to look around.

I had regularly attended talks sponsored by the libertarian Cato Institute in midtown Manhattan, and I often relied on its work in my own writing. On its website one evening, I clicked on "Jobs at Cato" and found that it was looking for a fundraiser. The job had nothing to do with writing about economics, but I sent in my résumé.

Soon enough, I was in Washington, D.C., interviewing with Cato's co-founder Ed Crane. We hit it off, and he's been an influential friend ever since. He wasn't interested in my writing, but he thought I'd do well with the institute's top donors. Crane offered me a job, and I took it, a decision that had my friends and family wondering. Not all that long ago I had been working at Goldman Sachs, and now I was fund-raising for a nonprofit? It sure looked like my career had been grounded.

But I had a plan (and bills to pay). I would continue to write, albeit on the side. Meanwhile, I believed in Cato's mission, and they were going to pay me to talk policy with highly successful and generous people. The visits were amazing. I learned a great deal from these people, who educated me in ways that college and business school never could. In fact, my second book, *Who Needs the Fed?*, was inspired by my conversations with Cato donor Hall McAdams. I dedicated the book to him.

Around the time that I arrived at Cato, Eliot Spitzer, then the New York attorney general, launched a Wall Street witch hunt. The Internet boom, like all booms, left a lot of failures in its wake. Eager to build a national reputation out of a normal market correction, Spitzer set about attacking analysts who had promoted ill-fated Internet stocks and went after mutual funds that allowed "market timers" to move in and out of mutual funds. I knew from my time at Goldman Sachs that Spitzer's attacks were baseless, and I wrote an opinion piece calling him out. Alan Reynolds of Cato liked it and sent it to *National Review*, where it ran online.

Here I note a happy irony in my story. The collapse of Internet stocks ended my time at Goldman, but the rise of the Internet presented huge new opportunities to writers. No longer confined to the limited space of printed newspapers and magazines, writers with a point of view now had unlimited space for expression. The Internet was unknown when I graduated from college, but by 2003, it was ready with an opening for me. When *National Review Online* posted my first public op-ed, I was a changed person.

After that opinion piece on Spitzer, I gradually migrated to economics op-eds. Raising funds from Cato donors was fun, but writing policy pieces was my passion. I'd work a full day for Cato and then write well into the night. Weekends included a lot of writing too. It's easy to go into the office on weekends when you feel elevated by what you're doing. I finally understood why Goldman Sachs investment bankers were willing to work the horrible hours that they did. While the handsome compensation surely factored into it, deal-making reinforced their talents in the way that I felt writing did mine. I couldn't get enough of it.

None of this was easy, and sometimes it was embarrassing. At a party with my parents, people asked me what I was doing. I told them fundraising, but my mom added quickly that I also wrote op-eds. That stung. My parents obviously didn't take the fundraising work seriously, but they were proud of the writing.

By 2005, I was fairly regular at both *National Review Online* and the now defunct *TechCentralStation*. It was a dream, and I'm forever grateful to Chris McEvoy (*National Review*) and Nick Schulz (*TechCentralStation*) for giving me a chance to opine on economics as "a writer based in Washington, D.C." Cato wasn't interested in employing me as a policy analyst, and no one else seemed to be either. That stung too, but if you're doing what you love it's important to embrace the snubs. That's what I did. If no one thought me worthy, I'd prove them wrong.

The more I wrote, the more notice I achieved. In 2006, one of my heroes, Steve Forbes, cited me as a "monetary expert" in his influential magazine column.[3] Not long after that, David DesRosiers of the Manhattan Institute asked me to consider succeeding him as director of fundraising there. It was flattering, but I told him that my next job would be as a policy writer. It turned out that the Manhattan Institute was helping to launch RealClearMarkets.com—a companion site to the successful RealClearPolitics—and they were looking for an editor. I was hired a week later. It was difficult to leave Cato, but this was the chance I'd been waiting for.

I began working at RCM in January 2007, and the site went live in November. Now I could comment on economic and market developments right away. No more waiting for an editor's decision. I wrote three columns most weeks. That's a lot, but it wasn't work. It was what I was born to do.

In the summer of 2008, Forbes, Inc., bought nearly a half share of RealClearHoldings, joining it with a globally established brand. Two summers later, I was called up to Forbes's impressive Fifth Avenue headquarters in New York. They were interested in making me full-time there. The interviews went well, and an offer was extended.

And yet I turned it down. My reservations were rooted in the Internet, which had made my writing work possible but had thrown the media business into uncertainty. By 2010, I was not only editing RealClearMarkets but was re-affiliated with H. C. Wainwright, was a senior economic adviser to Toreador Research & Trading, a small mutual fund company, and was back at the Cato Institute part time doing fundraising. Forbes expected me to give up all of those jobs for one. I wasn't ready to do that.

A week later, Steve Forbes himself called me. He said they needed me as opinions editor for the online version of *Forbes*. If allowed to maintain my other work, would I take it? He also stressed that it wouldn't get in the way of my eventually writing books. The answer was easy. I started in October 2010. It was time-consuming, but also a blast. I was charged with bringing in top economics and policy writers as *Forbes* contributors, so it was an interesting challenge.

By 2013, I had switched to political economy editor at *Forbes*. I had a little more free time, and my fiancée, Kendall, was needling me about writing a book. While I worked all or part of seven days a week doing what I truly loved, I often spent Saturdays at an independent movie theater. Why was I spending so much time at the movies, she wondered, instead of writing a book? She had a point, so I got started on the book, spending nearly every weekend from January to the end of March in the office.

George Orwell said that writing a book is like struggling with a long illness, and the months leading up to my wedding were difficult. Writing op-eds is fun, but books are terrifying. Working on something so much bigger than an op-ed, I feared that the result would be disappointing. And that's the point. I was able to write a book, and suffer the brutal hours, because writing is what I love to do.

Investment bankers can spend seven days a week in the office, football coaches and players can be in the film room all week, and writers can produce books because they're getting to express their unique skills. Doing what animates your talents isn't always going to be fun, but nothing worthwhile in life is easy.

About a week before my wedding, I completed what became *Popular Economics*, about a month later I had an agent, and not long after that I had a publisher, Regnery. In March 2015, George Will reviewed my book, calling me "a one-man antidote to economic obfuscation and mystification."[4] All those years of hard work had finally paid off. I'd begun writing for the public in 2003 as "a writer based in Washington, D.C." By 2015, I had a book out that received a lot of good notice. Since then I have moved from the Cato Institute to the Reason Foundation and then to FreedomWorks, all the while working with major donors.

It has been quite a ride—exciting, occasionally tense, and rarely what I expected. The biggest surprise was the rise of the Internet, which made it far easier for me to write for the public than it would have been in the more primitive economy of the twentieth century.

My struggles at Goldman Sachs and Credit Suisse forced me to think about what I really wanted to do. You shouldn't shrink from trying different things. All work is education, and a day rarely goes by when I don't make use in my writing of what I learned on Wall Street. Fear of the unknown, of losing my various jobs, moved me to write a book. My wife thinks I work too much, but I keep telling her that it's not work. It took me a while, but I finally found work that it would pain me *not* to do.

I'm not alone. *USA Today* reported in 2016, "Getting American workers to power down is an uphill battle." Indeed, "More than half of working Americans did not use all their time off in 2016."⁵ That's a beautiful problem. It indicates that amid America's growing prosperity, more of us are doing what we love. We can't not work.

When Alexis de Tocqueville toured the United States in the 1830s, he found us to be "restless in the midst of abundance."⁶ Perhaps Americans are consumed by work because we're descended from immigrants—people who had the "get up and go" to get up and go to a land of personal and economic freedom.

There's a strong correlation between economic freedom and economic growth, as China has demonstrated in recent decades. When an economy grows, more people can make a living doing what they love. Americans are known as being industrious because this is the country where a person's job is most likely to match his talents.

A young Andrew Carnegie wrote to an uncle in Scotland, "If I had been at Dunfermline working at the loom it's very likely I would have been a poor weaver all my days, but here, I can surely do something better than that, and if I don't it will be my own fault, for anyone can get along in this country."⁷ Carnegie nailed it.

Would you be a tireless worker if your only options were working long days on the farm or at the mill? That's what's so great about economic growth. The advances in productivity in rich countries continue to erase traditional forms of toil while expanding the range of new jobs. Hard work made the United States a rich country, and that wealth has produced the opportunities for more Americans to combine work with passion.

In the next chapter we'll consider the policies and thinking necessary for that growth to continue.

CHAPTER EIGHT

The "Venture Buyer"

"Whenever capital is withdrawn from production,
or from the fund destined for production, to be lent to the
State and expended unproductively, that whole sum is
withheld from the laboring classes."[1]
—John Stuart Mill

On July 3, 2016, the U.S. Senate announced that it was making the switch from BlackBerry smartphones to the more popular Android and iPhone versions. As *USA Today* remarked, it was a change "most of us made years ago."[2]

The Senate's archaic smartphone policy speaks volumes about the problem with government spending: it's very *conservative*. Governments spend money on what is known, as opposed to what will eventually be known.

Three weeks after the Senate announced its smartphone switch, Apple reported that its quarterly profits had fallen 27 percent, admitting that slower iPhone sales were a big part of the reason.[3] While iPhone sales were dropping, Apple's Chinese rival Huawei Technologies enjoyed a major surge in sales of its own smartphone, challenging the giants Samsung and Apple. The same week that Apple announced its falling profits, Huawei projected that it would ship 140 million smartphones in 2016, a 30 percent jump from the previous year.[4] Profits always attract competition.

Will Huawei eventually knock Apple and Samsung off of their lofty perch? It's impossible to know. The most successful investors earn billions because they are able to see into the future correctly—sometimes. You never know, but the iPhone could be yesterday's news at some point. Figure that we've seen this before.

At one time, BlackBerry was king of the smartphone hill. In 2005, National Public Radio decreed the BlackBerry "a must-have gadget, a wireless hand-held computer that can send e-mail and make phone calls,"[5] and compared it to the Palm Treo. Heard anything about *that* recently?

To be fair, when NPR reported on the BlackBerry, it was the dominant product. No one was thinking that a computer or Internet company might produce a marketable smartphone. Palm's CEO observed in 2006, "We've learned and struggled for a few years here figuring out how to make a decent phone. PC guys are not going to just figure this out. They're not going to just walk in."[6]

Microsoft's CEO Steve Ballmer was no more prescient. In January 2007, he asked mockingly about the coming wave of phones, "Five hundred dollars? Fully subsidized? With a plan? I said that's the most expensive phone in the world and it doesn't appeal to business customers because it doesn't have a keyboard, which makes it not a very good e-mail machine."[7]

A couple of months later, the computer industry pundit John Dvorak said, "Apple should pull the plug on the iPhone" since there was "no likelihood that Apple can be successful in a business this competitive." Dvorak concluded that first-mover advantage had closed the market for new entrants: "This is not an emerging business. In fact it's gone so far that it's in the process of consolidation with probably two players dominating everything, Nokia Corp. and Motorola Inc."[8]

BlackBerry's own CEO, Jim Balsillie, was just as complacent back in 2007: "The recent launch of Apple's iPhone does not pose a threat to

Research In Motion Ltd.'s consumer-geared BlackBerry Pearl and simply marks the entry of yet another competitor into the smartphone market."[9]

As the history of smartphones shows, no one knows the future. Not even the best minds in technology know with any certainty what's ahead. Could Huawei or some other lightly regarded entrant knock Apple out of the smartphone market? Definitely. So while the U.S. Senate is switching its allegiance to iPhones and Androids, the smartphone ground continues to shift.

Why does this matter? Because the federal government is not purchasing just iPhones. As *USA Today* notes, it has "more purchasing power than any other buyer in the world." In 2014 alone, the federal government awarded more than $445 billion in contracts to private sector suppliers.[10]

That spending power is the direct result of the enormous productivity of the American worker. While government can theoretically "print" dollars to spend, those dollars have purchasing power only to the extent that they're backed by the productivity of you and me. That is to say, the federal government could spend that $445 billion in 2014 only because the American people had 445 billion *fewer* dollars to spend that year.

Now, you may have a generally favorable or unfavorable view of government spending, depending on your politics, but the point I want to make here is that government spending blunts the expression of consumers' desires. We get up and go to work each day so we can exchange the fruits of our labor for what we desire but don't have. Our purchasing is a message to the market about those desires. Government spending necessarily diminishes that message.

In our consumption of goods and services, all of us are message-senders. But there's a particular kind of consumer who plays a critical role in the economic evolution that is transforming work. I call that consumer a "venture buyer." While a venture capitalist provides funds to a young and unproved business in exchange for an ownership share, a venture *buyer* is willing to try new products and services that are still unproved, and he's willing to pay a premium to be among the first to try them. Bloated government spending hinders the venture buyer, depriving entrepreneurs and businesses of vast amounts of market knowledge.

The venture buyer shows up in the stories of all kinds of products that we have come to take for granted. Consider the laser printer, a device now commonly found in American homes. You can buy one today for less than a hundred dollars, but not so long ago a laser printer was a fancy piece of high-tech equipment costing $17,000.[11] The only people who had them in their homes were the rich, who acted as the test market for what eventually proved desirable to us all.

On May 25, 1989, the first Magellan GPS portable navigation devices went on the market. These space-age gadgets weighed 1.5 pounds and cost three thousand dollars.[12] Thanks to the venture buyers of the nineties, GPS systems are now standard on the iPhone and Android, and free apps like Waze not only get you from point A to point B but also guide you around the traffic jams.

In 1970, Texas Instruments released the first pocket calculator, and those at the front of the line paid four hundred dollars for the miraculous gizmo.[13] Today you can access a calculator for free by entering "calculator" in the Google search bar. A few years earlier, IBM had introduced its first mainframe computers. The price of the simplest version was more than a million dollars.[14] Today, exponentially more powerful computers can be had for less than two hundred dollars.

In 1999, most people hadn't heard of wireless Internet, or "Wi-Fi." Bret Swanson, the head of Entropy Economics, recalls that the maximum capacity of Wi-Fi then "was 11 megabits per second. By 2003, when it started to go mainstream, the top capacity was 54 megabits per second. Today, it has surpassed 1 gigabit per second, or 100 times faster than in 1999 and 20 times faster than in 2003."[15]

As recently as the early 1990s, cellular phones were status symbols carried around by the rich. Motorola introduced the first one in 1983—the size of a brick, with lousy reception and a battery that lasted half an hour. This phone cost $3,995, and you paid through the nose for each call.[16] Despite the price, the rich proudly talked on them while the rest of us looked on in awe. Today, of course, we have vastly more powerful phones with computers, Wi-Fi, and built-in GPS, and the prices of these advanced gadgets are falling by the day.

These are just a few of countless examples that illustrate the importance of the venture buyer, sometimes called the "early adopter." Entrepreneurs hope to grow rich by being the first to figure out what consumers will want, but that's difficult because consumers often don't know what they want. No one was demanding computers, GPS systems, smartphones, or Wi-Fi before they were invented. Venture buyers dipped their toes into the water, and their purchases had a profound influence on how we live and work today.

Try to imagine our economy without computers, GPS, and mobile phones. Greg Milner, who has written the history of GPS, contends that this technology's "true economic influence" is so massive—in the trillions of dollars—that it "resists qualification."[17] He's right. For example, Uber, with its market capitalization of more than $60 billion,[18] is impossible without GPS and smartphones. And how many people are financing their education by driving for Uber?

Smartphones are a crucial part of Apple, the most valuable company in the world. Once again, thank the venture buyers. Without them, economic evolution comes to a halt and so do the dreams of those who want to match their passion and intelligence with their professional work.

That brings us back to the government. The more it helps itself to its citizens' disposal income, the less venture buyers have to spend. But spending is spending, isn't it? What difference does it make whether the government or private citizens act as venture buyers? It makes a big difference, actually. As the Senate's tardy switch from the BlackBerry to iPhones and Androids reveals, governments can't be early adopters. *It's too risky.* Economic evolution depends on venture buyers who risk their disposable income on the consumer goods of the future, along with countless other items that will be forgotten.

The federal government made use of private-sector technological advances to craft a primitive version of the Internet, but the Internet's commercial potential went undetected by its creators. The military developed GPS with combat in mind, but without private-sector risk-takers, no one would have heard of Uber.[19]

Politicians talk about running the government like a business, but the government isn't a business and can't act like one. Unlimited funds and the absence of a profit-motive make it difficult to kill what's not working. The money keeps flowing in no matter what. The situation of a private business is quite different. As Ludwig von Mises explains, "the wealth of successful business men is always the result of a consumers' plebiscite, and, once acquired, this wealth can be retained only if it is employed in the way regarded by consumers as most beneficial to them."[20] Consumers and businesses make mistakes all the time, but they correct those mistakes or find themselves corrected.

When governments spend in "size" fashion, the economy is deprived of the advances that power growth. Average workers suffer, because the variety of work available to them depends on booming economic activity. What were the options for a worker in 1900 compared with the options in 2000? What were the options in 2000 compared with the options today? Growth begets variety and with it the expanding opportunities for people to match their talents and passions with their work.

Venture buyers are also essential to our health and wellbeing. In December 2015, Jimmy Carter announced the disappearance of his brain cancer. The former president had obtained the new and enormously costly drug Pembrolizumab, which treats cancer by boosting the body's immunity.[21] Carter's medical version of venture buying helped pharmaceutical entrepreneurs take another step toward making this drug affordable for everyone.

History shows that the high prices of new goods—the goods that venture buyers are testing for the rest of us—invariably come down.

Falling prices stimulate desires for the new goods and services that are the occasion for new forms of work.

For instance, some people are terribly devoted to dogs. If disposable income is rising, there's a market for professional dog walkers. In fact, by 2016 dog walking had become a $907 million business employing more than twenty-three thousand people. Ryan Stewart of Queens, New York, earns $110,000 a year working twenty-five hours a week doing what he enjoys. "It's full-time pay for part-time work," he says. "I think everyone would want that. I'm doing something that I love, and I have time to go to school at night."[22]

Stewart knows one dog walker who earns $150,000 per year and another who earns two thousand dollars per week in thirty-five to forty hours. All that for taking care of pets. Stewart adds that foreigners stop to take pictures of dog walkers because it's still a very American profession. It's no surprise that this form of work would reach the world's richest country first.[23]

While some can't get enough of dogs and the outdoors, others love wine. The famous hotel Ritz Paris has just finished a two-year, $450 million renovation. The owners spared no expense as evidenced by room rates that start at $1,100 per night. But the Ritz's guests want more than fancy rooms; they want the best of everything, including wine. The hotel has accordingly stocked its wine cellar with fifty thousand different vintages, all of them curated by thirty-five-year-old Estelle Touzet, the hotel's sommelier.[24]

Yes, lovers of wine can now make it a profession. The 2012 documentary *Somm* follows four certifiable wine geniuses as they prepare to take the master sommelier examination, one of the world's most difficult tests. The candidates sip wines from around the world and with amazing precision identify the year, country, and region in which they were made, the best food pairings, and just about everything else.

There are only 230 master sommeliers in the world, and their extraordinary intelligence about all things wine means they're eminently employable. But not all sommeliers have the "master" designation, so it's not just the few who have been the beneficiaries of a booming economy that has turned what was once a hobby of the rich into a profession.

If anyone doubts that the consumption of the rich eventually benefits us all, consider this: Costco is now the biggest importer of French wines in the world. The giant discount retailer has directed its considerable buying power to wine. Annette Alvarez-Peters, Costco's lead buyer, is not a master sommelier, but she is the most powerful wine buyer in the world.[25]

The pay in the wine business is not bad. In 2014 the median income for sommeliers—a profession that likely didn't exist at all one hundred or even fifty years ago—was sixty thousand dollars for men and fifty-five thousand for women. Income for advanced sommeliers was seventy-eight thousand dollars, and for masters the median came in at $150,000. For consulting alone, introductory sommeliers charge $250 per day, while masters can command a thousand dollars or more.[26]

With its affluent readership, the *Wall Street Journal* employs car-mad reporter, Dan Neil, to write about the world's best cars. Neil's "job" in August 2016 was to travel to England to test drive the Aston Martin Lagonda, an exclusive "super saloon."[27] Years before Neil starting writing about cars for the *Journal*, Laura Landro was staying at the world's best hotels and reviewing them for the newspaper. Neil and Landro were forerunners of a new profession they're calling "influencers."

No one had heard of this profession a few years ago, but *Marie Claire* magazine's Jo Piazza reports that influencers can now make "serious bank" for posting their fashion and food likes on Instagram, Twitter, and other social media sites.[28] Kylie Jenner launched a line of cosmetics in 2015 and within eighteen months hit $420 million in sales with the help of 99 million followers on Instagram.[29]

You don't have to be a celebrity like Kylie to enjoy this lucrative, high-living career. There are no barriers to entry. Giant cosmetics companies are starting to notice what I call "pajama entrepreneurs." The *New York Times* reports, "Some cosmetic companies have flown groups of influencers to Bora Bora; Necker Island, the private enclave of Sir Richard Branson in the British Virgin Islands; and Kauai in Hawaii for lavish, all expense paid vacations. In exchange, most influencers agree to post a certain number of YouTube videos or Instagram posts about the company's products."[30]

Chiara Ferragni, the thirty-year-old founder of the influential blog The Blonde Salad, is arguably the queen of this modern profession, which exists solely because the people who populate our increasingly prosperous planet are interested in what she and other influencers wear. Ferragni employs some fourteen people for a blog that generates revenues in excess of seven million dollars annually.[31]

Generating billions of dollars' worth of fashion sales, Ferragni and other influencers have become so important that they are now ranked in tiers. According to Piazza, many of the top-tier influencers have become so expensive that opportunities have emerged for the mid-tier, who have "only" a million Instagram followers. Even if you have only twenty-five thousand followers interested in what you wear, you might command two thousand dollars for each post, supplementing your income with five hundred dollars for each hashtag.[32] In the connected and prosperous new world that technology has brought about, people will pay you for posting what you're passionate about.

The venture buying of the rich sends crucial market signals to entrepreneurs about how the non-rich will be able to buy in the future. That the superrich generally get around on private jets suggests that someday we'll all fly privately. Better yet, venture buyers drive the economic evolution that will allow most of us to combine work, fun, and our unique skills and intelligence.

But reduced government spending is necessary for work to evolve from tedious toil to what it would pain us *not* to do. Government spending blinds the economy simply because it blunts the impact of the "venture buyers" necessary for growth. It also reduces our buying power such that there are fewer "I can't believe I get paid to do this" jobs like sommelier, dog walker, and influencer.

CHAPTER NINE

Why We Need People with Money to Burn

"We are all blessed by the genius of relatively few."[1]
—Warren Brookes

*"If you don't love something, you're not going
to go the extra mile, work the extra weekend,
challenge the status quo as much."*[2]
—Steve Jobs

You may be familiar with the rapper Armando "Pitbull" Perez because of his hit songs. But his music is only part of his story. The son of Cuban immigrants, Perez has extended his brand to fragrances, clothing, and even vodka—fairly typical ventures for an ambitious and energetic pop star. But his most interesting venture is not one you'd expect from a rapper: the Sports Leadership and Management charter schools—"SLAM!" for short.

The first SLAM! school opened in an impoverished Miami neighborhood in 2013, and others are open or planned in Tampa, several other Florida cities, Atlanta, and Las Vegas. "SLAM! is not about being a professional athlete," Perez explains. "It's about the business around it, teaching the kids you can be a physical therapist, an agent, a lawyer, a broadcaster. There's a whole business around sports."[3]

Perez's schools are designed to introduce youth to the expanding range of career possibilities in areas of interest to them. It's too early to know if SLAM! will achieve its goal of launching disadvantaged kids on satisfying and successful careers in sports and entertainment, but this ambitious project shows why wealth is crucial to the evolution of our economy. Rich people like Perez make experimentation possible, and without experimentation, there would be no economic progress.

The *Washington Post* once confidently asserted, "It is a fact that man can't fly."[4] Thank goodness the Wright Brothers not only ignored the naysayers but also had enough revenue from their bicycle shop to invest the considerable sum of one thousand dollars in their seemingly impossible aviation project.[5]

When the venture capitalist Ed Tuck set his mind to making GPS technology available to the general public, his search for investors led to eighty-six rejections before he found someone to help him bring Magellan GPS systems to market.[6] But consider the unseen. How many advances have never seen the light of day because the wealth to back them wasn't available?

It's hard to believe, now that Apple is the most valuable company on Earth, but when Steve Jobs returned from exile in 1997 to run the company he had co-founded, it was "less than ninety days from being insolvent."[7] Bill Gates, one of the world's richest men, invested $150 million in Jobs's return to Apple.[8] How many more investments might Gates have made, how many more world-changing companies might he have saved, how many more global problems might his foundation have solved with the billions that he and Microsoft have handed over in taxes over the years?

Amazon's billionaire founder, Jeff Bezos, was part of an investor group that placed $32 million with the start-up Uber back in 2011.[9] Uber, itself a direct result of previous investment-driven advances in smartphones and GPS, now employs tens of thousands around the world. Bezos, the world's richest man,[10] is an aggressive investor. Imagine how much more capital he could put to work if the tax man weren't constantly lying in wait.

Some people are ideologically committed to the principle that the rich should part with some portion of their wealth through taxes. I'm asking you to leave ideology aside for the moment and recognize that private capital matched with ideas is the most powerful engine of economic growth we know of. And economic growth is what produces the liberating new jobs that have enriched millions of lives and could enrich millions more. Untaxed wealth doesn't lie idle. It's either saved, directly invested in ways that put it in the hands of innovators, or spent on goods and services, giving more people the ability to match their work with their passion. Each dollar taxed away makes it marginally more expensive for the rich to invest their capital in risky new advances. Innovators need that capital because experimentation is *very expensive.*

Peter Thiel, the billionaire co-founder of PayPal and one of the original investors in what became Facebook, knows the perils of investing in the ideas of the future. In his book *Zero to One*, he explains that "most venture-backed companies don't IPO or get acquired; most fail, usually soon after they start. Due to these early failures, a venture fund typically loses money at first."[11] This is why much lighter taxation on existing wealth would benefit everyone.

With less of their wealth taxed away, the rich would have greater capacity for risks. The more they're taxed, the more careful they have to be with what's left to maintain their wealth. Indeed, taxes on the rich hurt those who aren't well to do much more than they hurt the rich themselves.

Thiel is a good example. He's constantly experimenting with new ideas. He even believes death itself can be cured.[12] But experimentation is enormously expensive, and the disappearance of common killers like cancer and heart disease will require gigantic investments. More money provides more chances to fail expensively on the way to success.

But what good are all of Peter Thiel's investments in technology for those of us who want to marry work and passion but find technology terrifying? Just remember how technological advances have ushered in a more economically advanced society overall. We hear all the time that technology is a job killer, and it's true that the automobile, computer, GPS, Wi-Fi, and smartphone have rendered plenty of old forms of work obsolete. But the prosperity wrought by technological advances has given us more jobs to choose from. Thanks to growth-inducing innovations, people without technological skills can pursue work that didn't exist when society was poorer. A hundred and fifty years ago, half of all Americans toiled on a farm.[13] I don't know many people who would go back to those days if they could.

Technology has indeed destroyed lots of jobs, but it has also freed almost every family from having to produce its own food. Without technological progress, your odds of finding work that matches your unique skills and intelligence would be greatly reduced. But that's not the whole story. The tradeoffs that technology has brought have been brilliantly advantageous for us all.

Technology improves our efficiency at work, our ability to meet and transact with people around the world, and even our health. It is only logical, then, that technological innovation drives enormous wealth creation as more and longer-living people interact with each other. And as wealth grows, so does demand for goods and services of all kinds that have little direct connection with technology. In short, the wealth that springs from technology is what Professor Enrico Moretti of the University of California at Berkeley calls a "jobs multiplier."

In *The New Geography of Jobs* (2012) Moretti asserts that "for each new high-tech job in a city, five additional jobs are ultimately created out of the high-tech sector."[14] As people prosper in tech, their need for other services grows—personal trainers, yoga instructors, investment bankers, lawyers, restaurants, wine...Since the average American spends 14 percent of his income on food and beverages, where there's abundant wealth there's the chance for the Wolfgang Puck or the Danny Meyer of tomorrow to pursue his passion alongside technologists pursuing theirs.[15] A rising tide in technological centers such as

San Francisco, San Jose, Austin, and Boston surely enhances opportunity for the majority of us not interested in, or intimidated by, technology.

Moretti finds that while Facebook's workforce numbers in the thousands, the apps that bring Facebook its hundreds of millions of visitors each day account for 53,000 jobs, while 130,000 new jobs are indirectly related to Facebook's success.[16] Likewise, Moretti calculates that the number of jobs for which Apple is indirectly responsible is five times the number of persons employed directly by Apple.[17]

For many people, their passion for their work depends on being their own boss. Moretti finds that most small businesses cluster around the large ones.[18] Big business makes small businesses possible because well-to-do workers need all sorts of services. Wealth begets new businesses and new jobs.

But aren't these high-tech businesses the preserve of the infamous One Percent? Don't they foster inequality, which we're constantly told is bad for the economy? To answer that highly-charged question, let's consider a revealing fact about human migration, which is a pure market signal. It's clear that workers eagerly go to where inequality is steepest because that's where the opportunity is. Danny Meyer is from St. Louis, but that's not where he starts restaurants (a single Shake Shack being the exception), because it's losing inhabitants by the day to places that embrace innovation and wealth creation.

The story gets even more interesting when we consider the contribution to economic progress of inherited wealth. Back in the 1970s, most households had only one or two televisions, and their viewing was limited to a few channels. In 1979, when Bill Rasmussen announced the launch of ESP-TV, the future *New York Times* reporter Bill Pennington thought, "This is the stupidest thing I've ever heard."[19] The venture that became ESPN sounded ridiculous. More to the point, ESPN almost didn't make it. Rasmussen took out a $9,400 advance on his credit card to keep the company afloat.[20] His son Scott emptied his bank account to pay the ninety-one-dollar incorporation fee.[21] As

Michael Freeman writes, the nascent sports network "was hemorrhaging so much some at the network feared it wouldn't survive beyond 1980."[22]

ESPN likely would have gone bankrupt but for the Getty Oil Trust. John Paul Getty, America's richest man in the late 1950s, left his family a huge fortune when he died in 1976. Eager to diversify the family's oil-based wealth, the trust invested $10 million in ESPN.[23] A network was born.

There are many arguments against the estate tax, but easily the most important one concerns capital formation. Taxes on estates shrink the amount of capital in search of entrepreneurs. The hidden result is an erosion of entrepreneurial risk-taking and an economy riding its brakes.

Supporters of the estate tax dismiss this argument as inconsequential. After all, the $10 million invested in ESPN was a tiny fraction of the Getty family's wealth. Even with a more confiscatory estate tax, they easily could have ponied up $10 million for this investment. Yet that contention actually clinches my argument. The Getty Oil Trust was happy to invest $10 million in this idea *because* it would feel no pain if the $10 million were lost. Would this investment have "made the cut" with a smaller estate? We will never know.

The Getty fortune's role in ESPN's rise is typical. The banking heir J. P. Morgan provided Thomas Edison with the initial capital for what became General Electric, a speculative investment that provoked his father's ridicule. The elder Morgan, writes the economic historian Thomas Kessner, "wanted to have nothing to do with the eccentric inventor and his bulb experiments."[24]

In 1924, Howard Hughes Jr. inherited his father's hugely successful Hughes Tool Company, giving him what the aviation historian T. A. Heppenheimer calls a "bottomless pot of money," which he used to purchase control of Trans World Airlines in 1939.[25] Telling those around him "I've got the money,"[26] Hughes invested in what became the Lockheed Constellation, a fast plane with a pressurized cabin that could fly above the weather.[27] Passenger travel by air became common thanks to inherited wealth backing risky ideas.

Nowadays high-risk, high-reward investing is the preserve of venture capital. Since most start-ups fail, as Peter Thiel points out, we need those investors with the capacity to lose enormous sums before they land on the rare success story. Indeed, inherited wealth was particularly crucial to Silicon Valley's rise. As Walter Isaacson recounts in *The Innovators*, "For much of the twentieth century, venture capital and private equity investing in new companies had been mainly the purview of a few wealthy families, such as the Vanderbilts, Rockefellers, Whitneys, Phippses, and Warburgs."[28] Venrock, the Rockefeller family's venture capital vehicle, invested alongside Arthur Rock in Apple Computer.[29]

Technology is not the only field to benefit from the existence of inherited fortunes, of course. The institutions of high culture—symphony orchestras, museums, and such—are obvious fruits of established wealth, but popular entertainment benefits as well. Megan Ellison, the daughter of Larry Ellison, the founder of Oracle, has taken her inheritance to Hollywood, producing such acclaimed films as *Joy, American Hustle*, and *Zero Dark Thirty*,[30] while Teddy Schwarzman, the son of the private equity billionaire Steve Schwarzman, has *The Imitation Game* and other films on his movie-production résumé.[31]

Because some have abundant wealth to lose, the broad economy gains. The vast amount of money backing all sorts of interesting ideas is producing exciting work. Some of these ventures will succeed, but most won't, and that's fine. Information, good and bad, is the source of economic progress.

It is easy to invest in what is known. The accepted strategy of wealth preservation generally involves allocation of capital to the stocks and bonds of established companies. That's how you and I invest. The Gettys or Ellisons can lose millions on a failed investment without feeling any pain, but it pains me a great deal to lose ten thousand dollars.

That's the chief problem with the estate tax. Apart from the economic distortions caused by efforts to avoid the tax, it forces heirs to invest what remains after taxes far more conservatively than they would do otherwise. A tax that intentionally breaks up fortunes forces heirs into defensive, as opposed to intrepid, investment stances. It's a risk killer.

The estate tax yielded $20 billion for the U.S. Treasury in 2003.[32] That's a small number relative to the economy as a whole, but it looms large when we consider what entrepreneurs might have achieved with even a fraction of that $20 billion. How much entrepreneurial experimentation was lost? How many information-rich failures never happened? Taxes on wealth, like government spending, are blinders on the economy.

The visionary George Gilder explains in his brilliant book *Knowledge and Power* that the "key to economic growth is not acquisition of things by the pursuit of monetary awards but the expansion of wealth through learning and discovery."[33] Gilder's essential point is that information, attained through risky entrepreneurial leaps and the unexpected, is the source of economic progress. The greatest drivers of modern prosperity—from the railroad, to the telephone, to the car, to the computer, to the jet, to the Internet (not to mention the medical advances that have doubled our life expectancy)—*were all surprises.* As the early technologist Howard Aiken once told a student, "Don't worry about people stealing an idea. If it's original, you will have to ram it down their throats."[34] Everything that's good seems silly until it's tried, and sometimes tried countless times.

Major innovations are suspect simply because they haven't been tried before. This fact, so important to commercial leaps—those of the past and those to come—leads to a lot of failures and to some successes. More than 99 percent of the two thousand automobile companies founded in the early twentieth century failed.[35] Nearly a century later, the vast majority of Internet start-ups vanished too.

Has the U.S. economy been weakened by all this carnage? Quite the opposite. Each era of innovation has been marked by intense experimentation that offered huge surges of information, producing inventions and ideas—all of them surprises—that transformed how we live. This is the source of the abundant range of jobs that is rapidly transforming work from an obligation to a passion.

While defensive investing for wealth preservation is a sensible goal for most people, it's not the source of intrepid entrepreneurial leaps that produce path-breaking innovations. Estate-tax apologists can point to a microscopic number of U.S. heirs who annually hand over $20 billion or so to the government, but they miss the unseen advances that this money could fund.

It's the wealth of the largest estates that, if not taxed, would most likely find its way to the riskiest ventures. When individuals and families have "too much" money to work with, their willingness to be experimental grows with each dollar that's not taxed away.

ESPN, much like the automobile before it and the Internet after, has been a wonderful surprise made possible by untaxed wealth finding its way to a new idea. ESPN employs more than four thousand sports-mad workers at its Bristol, Connecticut, headquarters alone.[36] We'll never know what other brilliant advances never saw the light of day because of punitive inheritance taxes that made heirs far more conservative in their investing. And that forces many of us who aren't rich to work rather than pursue our passion.

Besides encouraging the kind of investing that enlivens the economy, eliminating the inheritance tax would stimulate charitable giving. Arthur Brooks observes that "among families that give charitably, inherited income raises donations by about twice as much as other forms of wealth (such as money in a savings account or the value of a house), and more than four times as much as earned income."[37] Evidence supporting Brooks's findings can be found at nonprofits themselves. Many, including the Cato Institute, employ planned-giving experts whose sole focus is capturing wealth that the rich intend to leave behind.

Brooks adds that $50 trillion more is set to be passed on to heirs between the time he was writing (2012) and the middle of the twenty-first century.[38] If government taxes these transfers more lightly, the organizations that seek to solve society's problems would have a great deal more to spend.

Antipathy to taxes—whether income or estate—and government spending is usually regarded as a "conservative" position, but from the standpoint of economics, there's nothing ideological about it. It's a question of what drives economic development, government spending or private spending, and the answer is the latter.

Most people are not lazy, but many people *appear* lazy because they're in the wrong job. Economic growth is the path away from a life of job-generated misery and subsequent laziness, and economic growth comes from keeping privately created resources in the private sector and out of government hands. That's not conservative or liberal. That's reality.

If government spends and taxes less, venture buyers will inform entrepreneurs of what works, preparing the transformation of obscure luxuries into common goods. Reduced taxation of wealth will free up precious capital that can be directed to entrepreneurs, who will surprise us with commercial innovations that will improve our lives and make us healthier.

But won't eliminating the estate tax breed an entrenched and ever richer ruling class? Remarkably, 70 percent of the persons in the *Forbes* 400 list didn't inherit anything.[39] The quickest path to pushing today's *Forbes* 400 members off of the list is to let them hold onto every dime so that it can be invested in tomorrow's entrepreneurs.

Indeed, there would be no companies, no jobs, and no nonprofits if no one first created and preserved wealth. No ideology can get around that truth. So the path to the sort of jobs that combine work and passion is spending and taxing less. If politicians were to spend and tax substantially less, the future of work would be bright.

Chapter Ten

Love Your Robot, Love Your Job

"I don't really know what a vacation is. Usually, I'm so
interested in what I'm doing and where I am, every night
I'm making notes and keeping a record of it for myself.
It's like retirement: Some people look forward to retiring
[but] I can't imagine what that would mean."[1]
—Russell Banks, novelist and travel writer

In his endlessly interesting autobiography, *Open*, tennis great Andre Agassi explains the immense importance of a well-strung racquet. He would bring eight to each match, since "the string tension can be worth hundreds of thousands of dollars." Well, of course. In a prosperous world that can afford to pay millions of dollars to tennis players, the racquets with which they earn their living must be strung well.

Agassi didn't let just anyone string his racquets. He employed an "old school, Old World...Czech artiste named Roman." He continues, "So vital is Roman to my game that I take him on the road. He's officially a resident of New York, but when I'm playing in Wimbledon, he lives in London, and when I'm playing in the French Open, he's a Parisian." You get the picture. So did Agassi. Roman's stringing brilliance reminded him "of the singular importance in this world of a job done well."[2]

Roman is the beneficiary of the explosion of highly specialized work sparked by immense wealth creation, and he exemplifies the truth that we're happiest when we're working hard at what we do very well. Agassi's brilliance on the tennis court depended on other men's doing what they did brilliantly. While millions thrilled to Agassi's play, he relished "watching a craftsman" in Roman. Agassi intuitively gets the connection between free exchange and the specialization that frees us to do work that doesn't feel like work.

Which brings us to the great economic thinker Henry Hazlitt. When he wrote his classic *Economics in One Lesson* (1946), Hazlitt took the charts, formulas, and statistics that informed a lot of economics books and threw them out the window. Because he understood that economics is about human action, not numbers, he made simple and accessible what had previously been obscure to most.

Even though the text is available for free on the Internet, Hazlitt's seventy-year-old book still regularly ranks among the top 1 percent of bestsellers on Amazon. With good reason. It's an amazingly insightful read. Those who read it will know more about economics than 99 percent of credentialed, Ph.D. economists. It's that good.

I read it once a year, and my working copy is full of notes and underlining. My favorite passage, the one that I keep returning to, is this:

> What is harmful or disastrous to an individual must be equally harmful or disastrous to the collection of individuals that make up a nation.[3]

At first glance, that assertion may seem unremarkable, but it's arguably the most profound and informative statement in any economics book ever written. It's so powerful that if economists and politicians fully grasped it, our country and the world would be vastly more prosperous than they are. And more to the point, there would be little laziness in the world and lots of joy on Mondays. We would be so productive that the four-day week would be the rule. People would be doing the work they love, so it wouldn't be work.

I make three arguments in this book. First, everyone is intelligent in his own way. Second, everyone has a huge capacity to work if his work is matched with passion. Third, economic growth will allow work and passion to become one and the same for the greatest number of people. That's why Hazlitt's insight is so important. An "economy" is nothing more than a collection of individuals. When we take our economic thinking down to the level of the individual, we discover the secret to roaring economic growth: No individual is made more prosperous if local, state, and federal taxes shrink his income. What governments spend represents lost spending and savings for every individual.

Of course, we work for money. In the United States, we work for dollars. In Great Britain they work for pounds, in Europe for euros, in China for yuan, and in Japan for yen. The money we work for is what we exchange for all that we don't have. As individuals, we're not made more prosperous if the money we earn is devalued by monetary authorities. When they devalue for the sake of what they deem the "greater good," they vitiate the value of each worker's work.

And then there's trade. Absent it, we'd all be extremely poor. In my case, if I had to knit the clothes I wear, grow and raise the food I eat, manufacture the computer on which I type, and build the apartment in which I live, I would soon die unemployed, unclothed, unfed, and without shelter.

Thanks to trade we don't have to focus on work that doesn't match our talents. Instead, we can put our individual talents to work in the most remunerative way possible, then "import" from across the street and around the world all that we desire in return for our work. With free trade, we have the world's producers lining up to serve us, desperately trying to win our business, allowing us to devote our own energy to what *we* are good at.

Don't ever forget that an economy is made up of individuals. As individuals, we benefit from light taxation, money that holds its value, and markets open to trade. Those are the basics of economic growth.

What about savings? Economic pundits warn that if we don't spend enough of what we earn the economy will implode. They argue that consumption is the source of economic vitality. But that's a naïve error that comes from omitting the individual from their analysis.

Does saving money make *you* worse off? By definition, you're better off the more you save. Prudence rewards the individual. And by extension, what's good for the individual is good for the economy.

To see why this is true, we have to apply what's good for the individual to the superrich. I'm not going to pull any punches: If you want economic growth and the abundant work that comes with it, you need the rich, and you need them to save.

According to *Forbes*, LeBron James, Cam Newton, Kevin Durant, Phil Mickelson, Jordan Spieth, and Kobe Bryant are among the ten highest paid athletes in the world, with annual incomes ranging from $77 million to $50 million.[4] The highest paid celebrity is Taylor Swift, with $170 million in annual earnings; Howard Stern takes in $85 million, and Adele earns $80 million.[5] As for the richest people in the world, Amazon's founder, Jeff Bezos, sits at the top of the heap with a net worth of $112 billion, followed by Microsoft's co-founder, Bill Gates ($90 billion), and Warren Buffett ($84 billion).[6]

Whether it's James, Swift, or Gates, the simple truth is that none of them can spend all that he or she has. *And that's the point.* Precisely because they can't spend all that they've earned and saved, we all benefit. The savings that are good for all of us are also good for the rich. And their savings are great for us.

If these rich people put every dollar they had in the bank, the bank wouldn't put it in the vault and let it sit. It would lend it to people who need a loan for a car, for school, or to turn their business dreams into reality. If these rich people want to be more aggressive and grow their wealth faster, they might put it in the stock market. If so, their wealth would be redistributed to companies interested in expanding. As they expand, they'll need to hire workers, and the savings of the superrich will reach all of us in the form of higher pay, along with investment in production enhancements that will render us even more productive. When the rich save, our ability to earn more in a growing range of jobs expands too.

What if they get really aggressive? We're talking about staggeringly rich people who can lose money on investments without feeling the pain. In that case, they might place their wealth in a venture capital fund that would invest in a future Microsoft, Facebook, or Google. Alternatively, they could risk their wealth in private equity or distressed investments. That money might be redistributed to a business that is months from insolvency and desperate for a cash infusion, as Apple was in 1997.

When the rich get to hold on to their wealth, that wealth chases new ideas that will benefit the rest of us. That's how the free market works. For instance, consider Joel Trammell, a serial technology entrepreneur in Austin, Texas. His most recent start-up, NetQoS, sold for more than $200 million when he decided to move on to his next commercial pursuit. Trammell's passion is starting and building companies. In his book *The CEO Tightrope* (2014), he admitted to a weakness:

> I'll be honest: my track record for providing capital is not great. Raising money is hard. Over my career of leading multiple companies, I have talked to more than a hundred institutional investors and have reached a deal exactly once.[7]

Trammell's admission speaks volumes about the importance of leaving wealth where it's produced, as opposed to taking it in taxes. He ultimately employed professional financiers to find capital to build his businesses, which employed hundreds, but it's a safe bet that his capital-raising track record would have been better had workers of all stripes been able to keep more of what they earned. Taxation reduces the amount of capital available for businesses to form and expand. The more wealth that is kept in the hands of its creators, the more likely that wealth is to benefit the rest of us by being invested.

Governments discourage savings not only with taxation but also with bad monetary policy. Stable money is crucial to the wellbeing of the individual and thus for the economy as a whole. When savers, rich and poor, put their dollars, euros, or yen to work, they hope to get a return on them. But if monetary authorities are devaluing the currency, people are less likely to save and invest it.

Consumption is the easy part. We all have infinite wants, and we don't need economists and politicians to encourage us to consume. Consumption is fun. But savings and investment are what drive economic progress.

When governments devalue the currency, they make us more likely to consume, shrinking the available supply of capital for investment. If devaluation of the dollar had been the norm 150 years ago, the emergence of the tractor would have been slowed immeasurably. Maybe it never would have reached us at all. We know this because there are no tractors in destitute countries bereft of investment. Technological advances are the result of those with money choosing investment over consumption, but if currency devaluation is the rule then investment is a less compelling option.

Imagine how lazy many of us would be if agricultural work were our only way to earn a living, as it was for most people 150 years ago. Investment is the source of progress, but if taxes are high or the currency is being devalued, there's less investment. The resulting slowdown in progress makes it more likely that people will have to spend their days working for a living as opposed to living to work.

At this point, some people get worried. Sure, we're all glad someone invented the tractor, freeing us from a life of backbreaking agricultural toil. But isn't the investment in technology today a threat to people's livelihoods? Tractors are one thing, *robots* are another!

Lest we forget, tractors, cars, computers, washing machines, and ATMs are all robots of a kind. They're all labor-saving devices that have destroyed jobs. But instead of putting Americans in breadlines, they've expanded the range of work available. Today the Japanese construction company Daiwa House and the electronics company Panasonic are developing an advanced washer and dryer—the Laundroid—that will not only clean your clothes but fold them too.[8] Such a device would make some work redundant, but then all wealth-enhancing progress makes certain jobs obsolete. Thank goodness. Is anyone willing to give up the telephone or email to encourage jobs at Western Union and the Post Office?

We should embrace technological advances, not only because they make life easier but also because they lead to more interesting work. That's been the norm in the developed world. As prosperity grows, work opportunities of all kinds expand. But where technology is shunned, work options are limited.

By the way, the developed world's move in the direction of automation does not mean we're producing less "stuff." We're producing more with less. This is as much to our advantage as it was to produce more food with fewer people on the farm.

You often hear that Americans don't manufacture anymore, but U.S. factories produce as much as China's do, more than double what the Japanese produce, and many times what's produced in Germany and South Korea.[9] The automation of the factory has freed Americans to pursue higher value work at higher pay. New York and Los Angeles once ranked first and fourth among American cities in manufacturing.[10] They're extraordinarily rich cities today precisely because they're no longer at the top of that list. They've moved on.

American workers are far too valuable for factories. Some of this work has moved to China, where it pays the daily equivalent of a Starbucks latte,[11] but factories are leaving China too because the Chinese don't want to work in them any more than Americans did. Factory work is a political issue not because Americans yearn for the past but because they yearn for economic growth. A return of factory work to the United States would indicate falling wages and a decline in growth.

To understand the importance of robots to our economic future, recall Joel Trammell's search for capital. When he was seeking dollars he was actually seeking what dollars could be exchanged for: office space, computers, desks, chairs, labor, etc. The robotization of the U.S. economy will provide abundant resources at low prices because robots can work all day, every day. That kind of productivity will open up abundant capital for the entrepreneurs and businesses of tomorrow. Cheap capital will make it easier to form new companies providing good jobs. And with backbreaking work consigned to the history books, the jobs of tomorrow will have a lot more to do with what interests us, as opposed to what merely feeds us.

Just as the tractor, car, computer, and Internet have fostered amazing wealth creation, the robot will too. There will be even more investment in the companies of the future, not to mention demand for athletes, chefs, musicians, and other entertainers in what will be a highly advanced society.

People used to work six days per week, and now five is the norm. What if Rob Rhinehart is correct about a four-day workweek in our future? If he is, then the amount of disposable income chasing leisure activities will skyrocket, and with it opportunities for actors, musicians, restaurateurs, and sommeliers.

Toward the end of *Economics in One Lesson*, Henry Hazlitt wrote about "the frequent assumption that there is a fixed limit to the amount of new capital that can be absorbed, or even that the limit of capital expansion has already been reached."[12] With justified contempt, Hazlitt remarked, "It is incredible that such a view could prevail even among the ignorant."[13] He elaborated:

> There will not be a "surplus" of capital until the most backward country is as well-equipped technologically as the most advanced, until the most inefficient factory in America is brought abreast of the factory with the latest and finest equipment, and until the most modern tools of production

have reached a point where human ingenuity is at a dead
end, and can improve them no further.[14]

America's problem is not too much capital or too much technology.
What's holding us back is *not enough robots* and, by extension, not
enough capital. If there were more, factories might be completely auto-
mated, but Americans wouldn't care, nor would anyone else, because
the economic resources that we call capital are always and everywhere
the source of progress that expand the range of jobs on offer.

In poor countries, where even primitive robots like the car, computer,
and washing machine are scarce, people have to work all the time with
little choice of jobs. It's in rich countries that people have a choice about
how they'll earn a living, not to mention how often they'll work. Americans don't hate Sundays and they don't hate work. The problem is a lack
of investment in the innovation necessary to expand the variety of work,
a problem caused by the government's confiscation of people's wealth.

If politicians and economists would abide by Hazlitt's maxim
about the importance of the individual, cutting taxes, freeing up trade,
and stabilizing the value of money, investment would soar. Even better,
it would build on itself. The more investment there is, the more wealth
creation—a virtuous cycle that leads to even more investment in companies capable of creating the exciting jobs of the future.

No one's lazy, but far too many are in the wrong job. If the political
class and the American people would stop penalizing wealth, if they
could see that the robot is the tractor of today, capital formation would
soar alongside amazing work that we won't dread resuming each Monday. That's the future if we'll allow it.

The good news is that a future without laziness has already arrived
to some degree in the United States. In the final chapter, you'll see why
that's true.

CHAPTER ELEVEN

Come Inside and Turn on the Xbox, You Have Work to Do

*"There's no such thing as being a professional poker player.
That's like being a drug dealer."*[1]
—Phil Hellmuth, World Champion poker player
($21 million in prize money), recalling his father's
reaction to his career choice

*"I hate to say it this way, but I never had a job.
I mean, I play golf. My parents were very good to me
and let me just play golf."*[2]
—Bubba Watson

I n August 2015, twelve thousand screaming fans packed Madison Square Garden. They weren't there for a basketball game or a summer hockey match pitting the world's best against each other. No, they were there to witness a *video game* matchup between Counter Logic Gaming and TeamSoloMid in a best-of-five series for the North American League of Legends championship. ESPN's SportsCenter was among the media covering the contest.[3]

Sports Illustrated profiled one of the contestants, twenty-two-year-old Peter "Doublelift" Peng: "Thin, bespectacled and wickedly smart, he's in some ways the stereotype of the gamer, having picked up the hobby as a young teen in San Juan Capistrano, Calif., looking to fill lonely afternoons." Peng turned pro in the nascent profession of video games at the age of seventeen, to the dismay of his parents. They had expected him to parlay his 4.3 high school GPA into a career in medicine, but Peng had different thoughts. His parents kicked him out of the house in response.[4]

Video gaming is this country's fastest growing leisure activity. Ninety-three million Americans are active in sports, and while that's not a number to sniff at, 194 million are active video game players. The explosion of interest has been so strong, reports *Sports Illustrated*, that "the kid you picked on in high school can now make upward of $1 million a year—in salary, prize money and sponsorship and advertising revenue—as a professional gamer."[5] Robert Morris University in Illinois fields a varsity League of Legends team, and the University of Washington is considering scholarships for gamers.[6] Foreign video gamers are issued P-1 athlete visas, and players can attain partial scholarships.[7]

Video gaming as a sport or profession, still in its infancy, seems poised for enormous growth. More people (27 million worldwide) watched the 2014 League of Legends world championship matchup between South Korea's Samsung Galaxy White team and China's Star Horn Royal Club than watched the title-clinching game of the 2014 World Series (23.5 million), the NBA finals (17.9 million), or the Stanley Cup finals (6 million). In 2014, Amazon purchased Twitch.tv—a streaming site for video matchups with more traffic than WWE.com, MLB.com, and ESPN.com combined—for $970 million. The 2013 League of Legends championship at the Staples Center in Los Angeles sold out ten thousand seats in less than an hour, while the subsequent world championship at Seoul World Cup stadium drew forty thousand attendees.[8]

Dennis "Thresh" Fong, the first professional video gamer, according to the *Guinness Book of World Records*, won a Ferrari 328 at a 1997 Quake tournament, a modest prize by today's standards. In 2015 the five-man Evil Geniuses team won $6.6 million in the Data 2 international championship. With his $1.3 million share, team member Sumail "SumaiL" Hassan became the first teen "e-sports millionaire."

Data 2 tournaments have handed out nearly $50 million in prize money to 1,248 gamers playing in 467 tournaments since 2011. With the purses growing and sponsorships from name-brand companies like Geico, Red Bull, and HTC, budgets for the major North American teams are in the three-to-five-million-dollar range.[9]

At this point, you've probably already guessed that the surging interest of fans and corporate sponsors in video gaming is having a "trickle down" effect. "Video game coach" is now a career for some. The *Wall Street Journal* reported in 2015, "Some e-sports coaches make between $30,000 and $50,000 a year." John Thorn, Major League Baseball's official historian, acknowledged that compensation for video game coaches is in line with that of minor league baseball coaches.[10] Imagine where compensation will head if the phenomenon grows.

If someone had talked about becoming a professional video gamer in 1972, when the Magnavox Odyssey was invented, he wouldn't have received even the polite expressions of faux interest that Danny Meyer received when he talked to friends and relatives about opening a restaurant in the 1980s. He'd have been laughed out of the room. But since the 1970s, much of the world has moved in the direction of the very economic freedom that always and everywhere rewards us with booming economic growth—growth that has stimulated the rise of fun professions that no serious person would have imagined forty years ago.

These new forms of work spring from venture buyers, venture sponsors, and venture investors with the means to try a little bit of everything. If all of us—rich and poor—faced substantially lower taxation, if government spending were substantially lower, new kinds of work would proliferate even more dramatically than they're already doing.

We have already seen how all kinds of careers are opening up in football, basketball, and baseball. Something similar is happening in golf. The New Zealander Steve Williams is the most successful caddy in the history of the sport. Having "carried the bag" for world-class players like Greg Norman, Raymond Floyd, Adam Scott, and Tiger Woods, Williams has 150 tournament wins to his name.[11] And in case you thought a caddy did nothing more than tote his boss's clubs around the course, bear in mind that his collaboration is so critical that players hand over 10 percent of their winnings to their caddies.

Ahead of each tournament, a caddy walks the course searching for danger spots in the rough, calculates yardage with great precision so he can advise his player about which club to use from each spot on the track, and in general searches for any edge that might benefit his player when the tournament begins. As Williams puts it in his autobiography, *Out of the Rough*, "A caddy's job is so much more than what you see on TV." A good caddy understands "a course's design and the type of shots [a] player is capable of playing in order to get around it in the most efficient fashion." A successful caddy "will also understand his player: how he performs in certain situations, how to get the best out of him, how to lift him up when he's down. A caddy is like a jockey on a horse, or a navigator in a rally car. In the same way a good jockey can be the difference in a close race."[12]

Jim "Bones" Mackay, Phil Mickelson's former caddy, paid homage to Williams's genius in an interview about the 2008 U.S. Open:

> We played the first two rounds with Tiger [Woods] at the '08 U.S. Open at Torrey Pines, which he famously went on to win.... I know for a fact just watching him and Steve Williams work together that day that Steve Williams saved him two to four shots, just in the two rounds we played with him.[13]

Woods won the tournament in a nineteen-hole playoff, but without Williams's steady hand, he probably wouldn't have made the playoff. Caddying is a remarkably cerebral endeavor.

Williams's father was an accomplished golfer himself and even had the option to turn pro with the backing of Wiseman's, a sporting goods retailer in New Zealand. He was put off by his father's telling him "there's no future in golf."[14] The golfing legend Arnold Palmer said that his future father-in-law "hated my ass" and skeptically asked his daughter, "You're going to marry a golf pro?"[15] He had a point. But economic evolution was at work, changing the ways in which people can earn a living. Palmer's father-in-law might have been less skeptical today.

Steve Williams focused his energy from an early age on sports. Uninterested in school, he regularly cut class, and by the time it was legal for him to leave school altogether, he did just that. He recalls that as a child, he "had no idea…you could be a professional caddy,"[16] but when he was paid $150 for carrying the bag for the legendary Australian golfer Peter Thomson, a light went on. Thomson thought Williams had the skill to be a professional golfer, but Williams demurred, "No, I want to be a caddy."[17] And so he became one when he dropped out of school at fifteen. By the 1980s, when he was in his twenties, disposable income and rising corporate profits had made golf a much more lucrative sport. With tournament purses on the rise, there was plenty of demand for the best caddies. Williams caddied around the world, finding that "players would often win soon after hiring me."[18]

Prior to the rise of Williams, Mackay, and other top professionals, caddies were mostly known for their capacity for alcohol, not to mention their playful nicknames, such as "Silly Billy," "Mustard," and "Goat." But when the pay went up, a once colorful hobby became a profession.[19] Williams "wanted to caddy, not party."[20]

Then came Tiger Woods. The massive wealth he generated for golf changed everything about the game. As Williams recalls,

> When I started, the prize pools were quite small by today's standards, but since Tiger Woods came along and prize money skyrocketed thanks to increased TV ratings, a professional can

earn over $1 million for a win, which means the caddy can pick up $100,000 for a week's work, or a 10 per cent cut of a player's earnings.[21]

Woods hired Williams in 1999, and the pair embarked on an incredible tear of eighty-four tournament championships. Soon enough the high school dropout was a rich man, accumulating so much wealth that he started his own charitable foundation and donated $500,000 of his own money to the Starship Children's Hospital in Auckland.[22] It's the virtuous cycle again—growth leading to higher-paying jobs and more giving.

Williams is now retired with a secure legacy as one of the greats. Hank Haney, Tiger Woods's former golf coach, has said that Williams's "record as a caddy is the greatest in the history of golf." Yet if he'd been born fifteen to twenty years earlier, odds are he would not have been able to turn caddying into a lucrative profession. It took the boom times of the 1980s to make that dream a reality.

The same could be said of Haney, whose coaching profession required prosperous times for it to evolve. He recalls wanting "to be a golf instructor from the time I was a teenager."[23] As Haney was growing up, "the best-known instructors built their reputations helping average golfers."[24] It was a living, but even Harvey Penick, the legendary teacher and author of *Harvey Penick's Little Red Book*, never traveled with top students such as Ben Crenshaw and Tom Kite.[25]

But once David Leadbetter corrected Nick Faldo's swing, launching Faldo on a string of six major championships, and Haney coached Mark O'Meara into a major-winner, the profession became rather professional. As Haney recounts, it drove "more tour players to seek full-time teachers; it led more instructors to travel the tour looking for business and developing stables."[26] The term "swing guru" became common. With all the money to be made in the sport, more people are able to turn what used to be a hobby or a passion into a career. And a cerebral one at that.

Haney contends that "Golf is what the ball does." After that, the *golf teacher* enters the picture. As he puts it, "the flight of the ball tells the teacher where the student's club was at impact. From there, the teacher can make appropriate corrections to grip, posture, alignment, ball position, plan, club path, or clubface angle."[27]

Tiger Woods paid Haney fifty thousand dollars per year for his services, a relatively low figure explained by the opportunities it opened up for the teacher.[28] Haney already had golf schools before he taught Woods, but now he's a global instructor. It's his obsession, and that's the point. Haney asserts that "anybody who is really successful at anything has an incredible passion that is basically an obsession. My mother and my sister used to complain that all I ever talked about was golf, that all I ever wanted to do was practice."[29] Absolutely. But let's not forget that had Haney grown up in a country where economic activity was restrained, he would never have been able to pursue his passion. Work that is combined with obsession is an effect of freedom and economic growth. Always.

Once upon a time, frequent golfing was the reward for a life of "real work." Nowadays, golf, like football, basketball, and video gaming, can be a career. This truth is one of the great endorsements of economic growth. There aren't career options like this in Peru.

Of course, not all of us who love sports have the talent to play them at a high level. Prosperity is taking care of that too. Ivy Leaguers run baseball teams by the numbers the way that CEOs run companies. Lance Thompson, an assistant head football coach for the University of South Carolina Gamecocks, has commented to me that lucrative pay for coaches is attracting people who didn't play football themselves. They're signing on as unpaid assistants in the hope of learning the game and eventually coaching it.

There's even room in sports for the non-athlete who "knows everything there is to know about sports."[30] As of May 2016, there were six investment groups dedicated to betting on games. The managers of these sports funds "are not gamblers but traders," reports *Sports Illustrated*.

"People who send money to them are not bettors but sophisticated, aggressive investors seeking to diversify their assets and earn a high return."[31]

It's important that such activity be legal. Sophisticated investors have savings, or have clients who want a return on savings, and sports wagering is yet another way for them to put money to work based on extraordinary knowledge among investors as to what makes a win or loss most likely. We live in a wonderful world, and it gets better all the time.

We have already learned about dog-walkers, but there's much more to the pet business than that. Since, as the *Wall Street Journal* has noted, "pets enjoy new status in the social pecking order (think dogs with more Instagram followers than you)," some of them are getting to eat people food, particularly during the holidays. Flush pet owners are more likely to allow their dogs to eat as they do.[32] That might not be good for Fido, as the *Wall Street Journal* notes:

> The dog-obesity epidemic has spurred its own thriving cottage industry. There are canine diet consultants, personal weight-loss coaches, doggy fat camps, canine fitness boot camps and websites that celebrate the biggest losers. Dog fitness products monitor activity with GPS precision and plastic surgery can remove sagging skin after weight loss.[33]

That's an indulgence that could take place only in the midst of prosperity, and prosperity is the greatest reward of all. For fun, let's call it Tamny's Law:

Laziness decreases as prosperity increases, expanding the range of work options so that every person can do the work that most accentuates his individual talents.

As the economy grows, so does disposable income, and with it the savings and spending that drive progress. This holds true even in North Korea, where, the *New York Times* reports, the economy "is showing surprising signs of life" in the marketplaces bubbling up around Pyongyang. "[T]here are now enough cars on its once-empty streets for some residents to make a living washing them."[34] The arrival of those jobs in this most backward of cities perfectly illustrates the end of laziness.

Americans might not be impressed by new jobs at the car wash, but in North Korea they represent substantial progress. The important point is that these new forms of work in the Hermit Kingdom are an example of what happens in the developed world each day. For every old job technology takes away, it gives all kinds of new jobs. Prosperity is the path to the end of laziness.

If you are unhappy or unsuccessful at work, it's not that you don't have talent, a work ethic, or intelligence. Everyone has the capacity to work hard if his work engages and develops his talents, but that kind of job will be harder to come by if the economy isn't growing as much as it could.

If we allow the economy to grow by letting people keep what they earn, preserving the value of the money they earn to encourage savings and investment, and allowing everyone to trade the fruits of his labor with anyone he wants without regard to national borders, will there be inequality? Without question. *Massive inequality.* Inequality is a feature of a growing economy, not a bug.

That makes sense if we focus our economic thinking on the individual. Is the NBA worse off because Steph Curry and LeBron James are the best players in the world? Is the NFL weaker because Tom Brady and Aaron Rodgers are much better passers than Matt Schaub and Mark Sanchez? Of course not. Without inequality, the NBA and NFL would be a bore, and there would be little opportunity for anyone to make a remunerative career in either sport at any level.

Is it a disadvantage to you individually that Paul McCartney can look at an instrument and almost immediately know how to play it? Are you worse off because Taylor Swift can turn life experiences into songs that the world wants to buy and sing along to? Are the blind who rely on Google Maps worse off because Google employs numerous millionaires and billionaires?

Steve Jobs died a billionaire, and Amazon's Jeff Bezos is worth tens of billions. Would you prefer that Jobs had been a layabout? Bezos, too? No, the world would be better and engaging work much more plentiful if there were hundreds of Jobses and Bezoses.

A more fundamental question is what will make you better off and happier in life, work that is least likely to elevate your talents, or work that isn't really even work because you enjoy it so much? The answer is easy. In an economy of individuals, we're all better off when each person gets to pursue what most amplifies his unique skills and intelligence. As individuals, we're all in pursuit of inequality. That's what makes us happy: doing work that elevates us as singular people.

Eric Ripert is a celebrity chef. Booming economic growth has allowed people like him to choose careers that accentuate their individual genius. In his autobiography, *32 Yolks*, Ripert recalls, "Food—shopping for it, making it, eating it—was my greatest happiness." And in describing the characters in kitchens today, he notes that the chefs have a "dangerous, rock star charisma that comes from those who are truly good at what they do."[35]

Pay attention to Ripert's words. He could be talking about you. The present doesn't define your future. You too could exude charisma and happiness, but only if you find the work that isn't work. It won't necessarily be easy, but imagine the satisfaction that will be yours if you can find what inspires you and makes you a star.

The United States is already becoming a nation of happy workers, but we've only scratched the surface. *The end of work* has in a sense already arrived, but it could be so much better if our government taxed and spent more sensibly.

You're not lazy, you're not stupid, and you're not bereft of talent. You, like so many others, simply suffer a capital deficit. That can change if we demand that it change. If that happens, a life of enriching work will be our reward, and a certain reward for our children.

ACKNOWLEDGMENTS

I n the writing of any book, the people, places, and sightings that influence the final product are endless. This was particularly true for *The End of Work*, mainly because any discussion of its theme invariably led to lots of excited talk about jobs that don't seem at all like work.

Still, a writer has to start somewhere. In this case, the idea for *The End of Work* came during a visit with my good friend Jeff Erber in Alexandria, Virginia, in 2015. He was generous enough to ask me to sign a number of copies of *Popular Economics* for his clients. As I signed, I referred to something I had recently read about the Beach Boys' front man, Brian Wilson. Apparently, this musical genius had almost no formal musical education. As Jeff and I talked about Wilson's otherworldly skills, I told him I'd like to turn the idea of combining work and passion into a book. While a book about the Federal Reserve came first, *The End of Work* was always on my mind. Big thanks to Jeff for encouraging it from the start.

I will never produce a book that doesn't have Hall McAdams's fingerprints all over it. For years, Hall had been discoursing on a variation of *The End of Work*'s theme. I'd like to think he'll agree that I took the knowledge he imparted to me about B. F. Skinner and ran with it. Hall and his wife, Letty, can expect lots of visits in the coming years as I shake them down for more book ideas.

Bob and Ruth Reingold have encouraged me every step of the way. Bob's experiences, especially in business, constantly inform my own thinking. As my wife, Kendall, would attest, I frequently quote Bob to explain why I'm doing something or why she *should* be doing something.

Ruth Westphal is a renaissance person. A successful business-woman, the author of a bestselling book about art, and a rather gener-ous supporter of the cause of liberty, she has never complained in my hearing about her treatment on the road to success. To Ruth, all entre-preneurs like her are discriminated against at first, and that's the point. Ruth will always be an inspiration.

David and Karen Parker have been supporting my writing for years. Their high-profile promotion of my books has meant a great deal. David gave me the ultimate compliment years ago when he told me my writing reminded him of the late, great Warren Brookes. I'll spend my working life trying to live up to that.

Bill Walton read an early manuscript of *The End of Work* and invited me up to his house to discuss it with cameras rolling. Bill's eponymous show, with its long-form approach, allows for deep discus-sion of the issues. In giving important subjects their due, Bill enhances the policy discussion, and a lot more. Thanks also to his wife, Sarah, for easing some of Bill's initial skepticism about my proposal that col-lege football players major in football.

John Batchelor is to radio what Bill is to web-based programming. In an increasingly bombastic media environment, John continues to stage serious conversations about serious issues. His long-standing support of my work is much appreciated.

George Will's *Men at Work* greatly influenced *The End of Work*, as anyone who reads this book will see. Not only did George write about the effect of rising disposable income on the nature of work, he also lived it. He viewed the writing of his incomparable book about baseball as the opposite of work, much as he delights in writing his columns. His encouragement of my writing over the years has meant more to me than he'll ever know.

Scott and Vanessa Barbee knew me from the early days when I was raising money as a job so that I could pursue what doesn't feel like work. Through the years their unceasing encouragement has meant a lot.

As he was for my first two books, Tim Reuter has been an invaluable sounding board and early editor. The great columnist Windsor Mann offered some useful examples about the explosion of jobs that don't feel like work. I very much enjoy reading Tim's and Windsor's writings, and can't wait for their books in the future.

Ed Crane made libertarianism a word and ultimately a movement. To this day, the Cato Institute that Ed co-founded employs dozens and dozens of passionate, energized scholars promoting freedom around the world. The work done at Cato that's an expression of passion is a model for this book.

Cato's former CEO John Allison always stressed the importance of "blood, sweat, and tears," and his powerful belief that hard work is the path to happiness has stuck with me. Indeed, it's a major theme in *The End of Work*. People doing what reinforces their unique skills have the capacity for endless amounts of toil, and lots of fulfillment as a result. Grit isn't enough.

Proving that assertion is the persistently impressive work in the field of hospitality performed by Jill Erber, Jennifer Ilecki, Kimberly Grant, and Anneli Werner. Each one of these women is eager to get to work every morning. I can't wait to see what their kids achieve in a world that's getting better all the time.

The End of Work was written while I was at Reason Foundation. Many thanks to David Nott, Julian Morris, Nick Gillespie, and Adrian Moore for their encouragement.

FreedomWorks is where I spend my days now. I remember well FreedomWorks' president Adam Brandon's excitement about a book that would reveal a largely unnoticed benefit of economic growth: jobs that we can't wait to get to. Adam, Parissa Sedghi, Jason Pye, and the whole FreedomWorks staff have been unwavering in their enthusiasm for what I do. I look forward to completing many more books with them. Their belief that the story of expanding prosperity requires real-world examples is what energizes me every day.

Regnery's Tom Spence edited *Popular Economics*, which means *The End of Work* is a reunion for us of sorts. While the mistakes are all mine, working with Tom has me certain that grammatical errors and mind-bending syntax will be kept to a minimum.

And then there's Steve Forbes. His kindness never ceases to amaze. Here's someone who's been changing the global policy discussion for decades, yet he still has time to read my columns and attend my speeches. I'll no doubt fail, but I'd like to be like Steve. My wife wishes the same. Indeed, in addition to teaching me endless amounts over the years, he's the nicest man I know.

Major thanks to my parents, Peter and Nancy, for not losing faith in me as my career took what may have seemed like a strange turn. There was a purpose in all this. *The End of Work* is very much my story. As for Kim Tamny, the sister I don't deserve, I'd like to think she's been looking forward to Mondays since at least the late 1990s, when she went to work at the Academy of Motion Picture Arts and Sciences.

Which brings me to my wife Kendall, and our baby daughter, Claire. Kendall, thank you for being a very regular source of ideas behind *The End of Work*. Your own reading very much informed this book, and as I see it, gave life to its message. At the same time, thank you for putting up with me during the writing of it. While work that doesn't feel like it is an amazing thing, sometimes it's just work. And it can be terrifying. Thank you, for being there for me amid all of my worrying. Most important, it's no exaggeration to say that without you, there quite simply are no books. Without your endless encouragement, I'd likely still be satisfied writing op-eds. What I owe you can't be quantified, but it's endless. And I'll spend all my days trying to repay what you've done for me.

As for Claire, this book is for you. It was completed just a few weeks before you entered the world. Thank you for bringing your mother and me so much joy ever since. I'm thrilled that when you finish school, you'll rarely dread Mondays. Thanks to persistent economic progress, your future won't be filled with anxiety. In fact, the only unease you'll experience will be over which talent you choose to express in the marketplace.

Introduction

1. Hyman G. Rickover, "Notable & Quotable," *Wall Street Journal*, September 16, 2015.

2. Keith Richards, *Life* (Boston: Little, Brown and Company, 2010), p. 490.

3. "Michael Jordan. How Important Is Practice?" 1991 Nike Ad. YouTube, 2:32. Posted December 2013. https://www.youtube.com/watch?v=hXdj8scRdFE.

4. Dan McCarney, "Quote history of Kobe: The Work Ethic," *NBA.com*, April 11, 2016.

5. Warren Buffett, "Better than Raising the Minimum Wage," *Wall Street Journal*, May 22, 2015.

6. Anupreeta Das, "Buffett's Lucky Billionaires Club," *Wall Street Journal*, October 22, 2015.

7. Andy Kierz, "Here's how rich you'd be if you had bet $1,000 on Warren Buffett way back when," *Business Insider*, March 2, 2015.

8. Peter Economy, "17 Remarkable Buffett Quotes that Will Inspire You to Remarkable Success and Happiness," Inc.com, July 30, 2015.

Chapter One: Why College Football Players Should Major in College Football

1.   Peter King, *Inside the Helmet* (New York: Simon & Schuster, 1993), 12.

2.   Matthew Futterman, "The Draft Prospect Out of Central Casting," *Wall Street Journal*, April 25, 2017.

3.   Andy Staples, "Decision 2016," *Sports Illustrated*, May 2, 2016.

4.   Tom Gerenger, "How Much Money Do NFL Players Make?"*MoneyNation*, January 5, 2016.

5.   Brent Shrotenboer, "The NFL's super plan to get even bigger," *USA Today*, January 31, 2014.

6.   Kurt Badenhausen, "The Dallas Cowboys Head The NFL's Most Valuable Teams at $4.8 Billion," *Forbes*, September 18, 2017.

7.   "Football Wins Again," *Sports Illustrated*, March 21, 2016.

8.   Brian Billick and Michael MacCambridge, *More Than a Game: The Glorious Present—and Uncertain Future—of the NFL* (New York: Scribner, 2009).

9.   King, *Inside the Helmet*, 24

10.   Dan Patrick, "Just My Type," *Sports Illustrated*, September 26, 2016

11.   King, *Inside the Helmet*, 32.

12.   Ibid., 33.

13.   Pete Thamel, "Who Dak?" *Sports Illustrated*, October 17, 2016.

14.   Greg A. Bedard, "Ch-Ch-Ch-Ch- Changes," *Sports Illustrated*, January 25, 2016.

15.   Jenny Vrentas, "The New Reality," *Sports Illustrated*, September 19, 2016.

16.   King, *Inside the Helmet*, 84.

17.   Ibid., 104.

18.   Ibid., 92.

19.   Ibid., 113.

20.   Andy Benoit, "Rob Gronkowski, Football Mastermind," *Sports Illustrated*, September 19, 2016.

21.   Greg A. Bedard, "College vs. Pro," *Sports Illustrated*, April 18, 2016.

22.   Ibid.

23.   Ibid.

24. Ibid.

25. Alan Siegel, "The top schools that have produced the best NFL players," *USA Today*, October 10, 2015.

26. Billick and MacCambridge, *More Than a Game*.

27. Ibid.

28. Jimmy Boyd, "Who Are the Highest Paid NFL Coaches & What Are Their Salaries?" Boyd'sBets, January 17, 2017

29. "Right-Hand Man," *Washington Times*, January 15, 2004, http://www.washingtontimes.com/news/2004/jan/15/20040115-112529-5440r/.

30. Alex Dunlap, "How Much Money Do NFL Front-Office Executives Make?" *Bleacher Report*, May 15, 2013.

31. Steve Berkowitz, Christopher Schnaars and Brent Schrotenboer, "More coaches hit $3M mark," *USA Today*, October 27, 2016.

32. Erik Brady, Steve Berkowitz and Christopher Schnaars, "Wisconsin bucks coaching salary trend," *USA Today*, October 9, 2015.

33. Associated Press, "Alabama Approves Contract Extension for Nick Saban Worth $65 Million," *New York Times*, May 2, 2017.

34. Associated Press, "Jimbo Fisher gets 10-year, $75 million deal at Texas A&M," *USA Today*, December 4, 2017.

35. Ibid

36. Dan Woken, Steve Berkowitz and Christopher Schnaars, "Being Head Coach Can Mean Less Money," *USA Today*, December 10, 2015.

37. Associated Press, "LSU AD expected schools to seek out coordinator Dave Aranda," *USA Today*, January 4, 2018.

38. Ibid

39. Woken, Berkowitz and Schnaars, "Being Head Coach Can Mean Less Money."

40. Associated Press, "Alabama Approves Contract Extension for Nick Saban Worth $65 Million."

41. Chad Leistikow and Steve Berkowitz, "Iowa pays strength coach $600K," *USA Today*, August 23, 2016.

42. "Texas town Oks $63M for a high school football stadium," FoxNews.com, May 10, 2016.

43. Michael Adams, "Show Me the Money," *Austin American-Statesman*, June 18, 2014.

44. USA Today Sportsline, "Magic Number, 15" *USA Today*, July 20, 2016.

45. USA Today Sportsline, "MAGIC NUMBER–$174,107.65," February 2, 2016.

46. Jeff Sentell, "Alabama's high school football coaching salaries soar past $120,000, search for how much your coach makes," AL.com, April 26, 2015.

47. Dan Radakovich, "At Clemson, we're proud of our success," *USA Today*, December 30, 2015.

Chapter Two: Intelligence and Passion Don't Stop at Football

1. Lee Jenkins, "Class In Session," *Sports Illustrated*, October 28, 2015.

2. Alexandra Wolfe, "Weekend Confidential: Becky Hammon," *Wall Street Journal*, April 29–30, 2017.

3. Chris Ballard, "Revenge of the Nerds," *Sports Illustrated*, November 23, 2015.

4. Ibid.

5. Ibid.

6. Ibid.

7. Jenkins, "Class In Session."

8. Ibid.

9. Lee Jenkins, "The Giant Killer," *Sports Illustrated*, May 23, 2016.

10. Ibid.

11. Ibid.

12. Ibid.

13. Lee Jenkins, "LeBron's Time," *Sports Illustrated*, December 7, 2015.

14. Lee Jenkins, "A Simple Plan," *Sports Illustrated*, March 6, 2017.

15. Kurt Badenhausen, "New York Knicks Head the NBA's Most Valuable Teams at $3 Billion," Forbes.com, January 20, 2016.

16. Horran Cameron, "The 411 on Overseas Basketball: Is It Worth It?" Fansided.

17. Nick Bedard, "Highest paid Chinese players in the CBA," Basketball Buddha, January 20, 2015.

18. "NBA Head Coach Contracts," OtherLeague, http://www.otherleague.com/contracts/nba-head-coach-contracts-salaries/.

19. Crystal Henderson, "Top 10 NBA Assistant Coaches: What They Once Earned as Players," *The Richest*, January 23, 2014.

20. Steve Berkowitz and Christopher Schnaars, "Record cash flows to college basketball coaches," *USA Today*, March 30, 2017.

21. Steve Berkowitz and Christopher Schnaars, "At least 35 college hoops coaches in $2M-plus pay club," *USA Today*, March 31, 2016.

22. Robert Strauss, "Assistant Coaches Join the Millionaire's Club," *New York Times*, February 12, 2016.

23. Ibid.

24. Rebecca Salinas, "50 highest-paid high school coaches in San Antonio," *mySA*, December 17, 2015.

25. Ibid.

26. George F. Will, *Men at Work: The Craft of Baseball*, (New York: Harper Perennial, 2010), p. xiv.

27. Ibid., xx.

28. Ibid., xxvi.

29. Ibid., xxvii.

30. Ibid., 7.

31. Ibid., 13.

32. Ibid., 22.

33. Ibid., 30.

34. Ibid., 164.

35. Ibid., 209.

36. Ibid., 221.

37. Ben Reiter, "The Slugger & the Scout," *Sports Illustrated*, May 8, 2017.

38. Mike Ozanian, "Baseball's Most Valuable Teams," Forbes.com, March 23, 2016.

39. Bob Nightengale, "Defending champion Royals spread wealth," *USA Today*, April 4, 2016.

40. Barry Svrluga, *The Grind: Inside Baseball's Endless Season* (New York: Blue Rider Press, 2015), 84.

41. Jimmy Boyd, "Highest Paid MLB Managers", BoydsBets, February 12, 2016.

42. Tom Verducci, "Secret Decoder Kings," *Sports Illustrated*, March 28, 2016.

43. Ibid.

44. Ibid.

45. Ibid.

46. Svrluga, *The Grind*, 48.

47. Ibid.

48. Thomas Boswell, "Mike Rizzo is worth every bit the Nationals are paying him—and more," *Washington Post*, May 15, 2016.

49. Svrluga, *The Grind*, 42.

50. Ibid., 93.

51. Ibid., 131.

52. Albert Chen, "The Metrics System," *Sports Illustrated*, August 22, 2016.

53. Bob Nightengale, "Dodgers Front Office Sets Stage For Success," *USA Today*, August 15, 2017.

Chapter Three: Education Isn't Meaningless, But It's Grossly Overrated

1. Ludwig von Mises, *Socialism: An Economic and Sociological Analysis* (Liberty Classics, 1981), 165.

2. Kent Hartman, *The Wrecking Crew* (New York: Thomas Dunne Books, 2012), 152.

3. Ibid., 153.

4. Ibid., 155.

5. Ibid., 154.

6. Ibid., 12.

7. Ibid., 13.

8. Ibid., 12.

9. Ibid., 13.

10. Ibid., 14–16.

11. Ibid., 42.

12. Bob Spitz, *The Beatles: The Biography* (Boston: Little, Brown, 2005), 8.

13. Ibid., 332.

14. Ibid., 337.

15. Ibid., 338.

16. Hartman, *The Wrecking Crew*, 152.
17. Bob Spitz, *The Beatles: The Biography*, 325.
18. Ibid., 87.
19. Ibid., 48.
20. Ibid., 108.
21. Ibid., 391.
22. Keith Richards, *Life* (Boston: Little, Brown, 2010), 40.
23. Ibid., 57.
24. Ibid., 58–59.
25. Ibid., 70–71.
26. Ibid., 77–78.
27. Richards, *Life*, 126–127.
28. Michael Keshen, "Top 9 Musicians Who Got Discovered on the Internet," Hover, December 4, 2014.
29. Ibid.
30. Hartman, *The Wrecking Crew*, 154.
31. Ibid., 52.
32. Ibid., 384.
33. Ibid., 325.
34. Richards, *Life*, 102.
35. Ibid., 103.
36. Ibid., 110.
37. Ibid., 241.
38. Jeffrey J. Selingo, "College Isn't Always the Answer," *Wall Street Journal*, May 27, 2015.
39. Jane Shaw, "Higher Learning, Meet Lower Job Prospects," *Wall Street Journal*, February 4, 2013.
40. Steven F. Hayward, *The Age of Reagan: The Fall of the Old Liberal Order* (Roseville, Calif.: Forum, 2001), 610.
41. Ibid., 610.
42. Walter Isaacson, *Steve Jobs* (New York: Simon & Schuster, 2011), 40.
43. Ibid., 102.

44. Mary Tradii, "Michael Dell," Encyclopedia.com, 2005, http://www.encyclopedia.com/topic/Michael_Dell.aspx.

45. David McCullough, *The Wright Brothers* (New York: Simon & Schuster, 2015), 35.

46. Brian Grazer and Charles Fishman, *A Curious Mind: The Secret to a Bigger Life* (New York: Simon & Schuster, 2015), 19.

47. Alexandra Wolfe, "Weekend Confidential: Peter Berg," *Wall Street Journal*, December 31, 2016–January 1, 2017.

48. Robyn Meredith, *The Elephant and the Dragon: The Rise of India and China and What It Means for All of Us* (New York: Norton, 2007), 34.

49. Paul E. Peterson and Eric A. Hamushek, "The Vital Link of Education and Prosperity," *Wall Street Journal*, September 11, 2013.

50. Nicholas Kristof, "The Educated Giant," *New York Times*, May 28, 2007.

51. Fox Butterfield, *China: Alive in the Bitter Sea* (New York: Times Books, 1982).

52. Ibid.

53. Tom Nagorski, "The Chutzpah of Jack Ma," *Wall Street Journal*, April 9–10, 2016.

54. George Gilder, *Wealth and Poverty* (New York: Basic Books, 1981), 99.

Chapter Four: What Was Once Silly Is Now Serious

1. Sam Kasner, "Both Huntress and Prey," *Vanity Fair*, November 2014.

2. Grant Achatz and Nick Kokonas, *Life, on the Line* (New York: Gotham Books, 2011), 4.

3. Danny Meyer, *Setting the Table: The Transforming Power of Hospitality in Business* (New York: Harper, 2008), paperback edition, 10.

4. Ibid., 9.

5. Ibid., 6–7.

6. Ibid., 20–21.

7. Ibid., 22.

8. Ibid.,. 26–29.

9. Ibid., 29.

10. Ibid., 30.

11. Ibid., 1–2.

12. Ibid., 35.

13. Ibid., 35.

14. Alexandra Wolfe, "Weekend Confidential: Wolfgang Puck," *Wall Street Journal*, March 26–27, 2016.

15. Ibid.

16. Achatz and Kokonas, *Life, on the Line*, 23.

17. Ibid., 27.

18. Ibid., 39.

19. Ibid., 288.

20. Ibid.,324.

21. Charles Passy, "Here's the Coffee You Ordered! Your Total Comes to $55" *Wall Street Journal*, October 17, 2017.

22. Danny Meyer, *Setting the Table: The Transforming Power of Hospitality in Business* (New York: Harper, 2008), paperback edition.

23. Julian Fellowes, *Snobs* (New York: St. Martin's, 2004), 123.

24. Roger Moore, *Last Man Standing: Tales from Tinseltown* (London: Michael O'Mara, 2012), 59.

25. Rob Lowe, *Stories I Only Tell My Friends* (New York: Henry Holt, 2011), 79.

26. Ibid., 80–81.

27. Brett Martin, *Difficult Men* (New York: Penguin Press, 2013, 239.

28. Ibid., 65.

29. Ibid., 268.

30. Ibid., 269.

31. Damon Darlin, "Falling Costs of Big-Screen TV's to Keep Falling," *New York Times*, August 20, 2005.

32. Dave Lewis, "Complete list of 2016 Emmy nominees," *Los Angeles Times*, July 14, 2016.

33. Josef Adalian and Maria Elena Fernandez, "The Business of Too Much TV," *New York*, May 18, 2016.

34. Ibid.

35. Tom Huddleston Jr., "These Networks (and Netflix) Dominated the 2016 Emmy Nominations," *Fortune*, July 14, 2016.

36. John Koblin, "With More TV Shows than Ever Vying for Eyeballs, It's Harder to Break Through," *New York Times*, January 8, 2018.

37. Adalian and Fernandez, "The Business of Too Much TV."

38. John Tamny, *Popular Economics* (Washington, DC: Regnery, 2015),189.

39. Bill Carter, *The Late Shift* (New York: Hyperion, 1994), 41.

40. Ibid., 44.

41. Jennifer Keishing Armstrong, *Seinfeldia* (New York: Simon & Schuster, 2016), 10.

42. Ibid., 201.

43. Luke O'Neil, "Could a College Degree in Comedy Be Anything Other than a Joke?" *New York Times Magazine*, June 13, 2016.

44. Lowe, *Stories I Only Tell My Friends*, 266.

Chapter Five: Abundant Profits Make Possible the Work That Isn't

1. Arthur C. Brooks, *Who Really Cares: The Surprising Truth about Compassionate Conservatism* (New York: Basic Books, 2006), xii.

2. Nikhil Deogun, "The Legacy: Roberto Goizueta Led Coca-Cola Stock Surge, and Its Home Prospers," *Wall Street Journal*, October 20, 1997.

3. Ibid.

4. Ibid.

5. Ibid.

6. John Tamny, "If Charity Is Their Goal, Gates and Buffett Should Hoard Their Wealth," Forbes.com, June 17, 2010.

7. Source: Bill & Melinda Gates Foundation Fact Sheet, http://www.gatesfoundation.org/Who-We-Are/General-Information/Foundation-Factsheet.

8. Deepa Seetharaman, "Zuckerberg Fund to Invest $3 Billion," *Wall Street Journal*, September 22, 2016.

9. Sarah Frier, "Mark Zuckerberg Philanthropy Pledge Sets New Giving Standard," *Bloomberg*, December 1, 2015.

10. Robert Arnott, William Bernstein, and Lillian Wu, "The Myth of Dynastic Wealth: The Rich Get Poorer," *Cato Journal*, Vol. 35 (Fall 2015): 461–463.

11.   Arthur C. Brooks, *Who Really Cares*, 3.

12.   Ibid.,

13.   Ibid., 7.

14.   Ibid., 77.

15.   Ibid., 78.

16.   Ibid., 124.

17.   Blair Tindall, *Mozart in the Jungle: Sex, Drugs and Classical Music* (New York: Atlantic Monthly Press, 2005),149.

18.   Ibid., 50.

19.   Ibid., 50.

20.   Ibid., 53–54.

21.   Ibid., 154.

22.   Ibid., 208.

23.   Ibid., 22.

24.   Ibid., 86.

25.   Ibid., 97.

26.   Ibid., 209.

27.   Ibid., 304.

28.   Monte Burke, "College Coaches Deserve Their Pay," *Wall Street Journal*, August 30, 2015.

29.   Ibid.

30.   Ibid.

31.   Ibid.

32.   Brooks, *Who Really Cares*, 119.

33.   Brooks, *Who Really Cares*, 139.

34.   Rebecca R. Ruiz and Jere Longman, "Brazil's Economic Woes Force Paralympic Cuts," *New York Times*, August 20, 2016.

Chapter Six: The Millennial Generation Will Be the Richest Yet— Until the Next One

1.   Alexandra Wolfe, "Weekend Confidential: Tony Bennett," *Wall Street Journal*, November 12–13, 2016.

2.   Robert Samuelson, "Why our children's future no longer looks so bright," *Washington Post*, October 16, 2011.

3.   Kevin Williamson, "Generation Vexed," *National Review*, November 17, 2014.

4.   Steven F. Hayward, *The Age of Reagan: The Fall of the Old Liberal Order* (Roseville: Forum, 2001), 581.

5.   Ibid., 575.

6.   Eric Hoffer, "Notable & Quotable: The Young," *Wall Street Journal*, June 2, 2017.

7.   Mike Isaac, "Upstarts Raiding Giants for Staff in Silicon Valley," *New York Times*, August 19, 2015.

8.   John Tamny, "Fear Not, Millennials Are Not Embracing Bernie Sanders Style Socialism," *Forbes*, August 3, 2016.

9.   Adam Shell, "In Quest for Millennials, Financial Firms Try to 'Crack the Code,'" *USA Today*, May 10, 2017.

Chapter Seven: My Story

1.   Dominick Dunne, *The Way We Lived Then* (New York: Crown Books, 1999), 200.

2.   Mark Bechtel, "Farewell," *Sports Illustrated*, December 28, 2015.

3.   Steve Forbes, "Powerful Antiterror Weapon," *Forbes*, October 6, 2006.

4.   George F. Will, "How income inequality benefits everybody," *Washington Post*, March 25, 2015.

5.   Charisse Jones, "Many Companies Force Workers to Use Time Off," *USA Today*, August 19, 2016.

6.   John D. Gartner, *The Hypomanic Edge* (New York: Simon & Schuster, 2005), 12.

7.   Ibid., 130.

Chapter Eight: The "Venture Buyer"

1.   John Stuart Mill, *Principles of Political Economy* (Amherst, N.Y: Prometheus Books), 100–101.

2.   Allana Akhtar, "U.S. Senate finally ditches Blackberry," *USA Today*, July 4, 2016.

3. Daisuke Wakabayashi, "Apple Sales Cool Off As Foes Heat Up," *Wall Street Journal*, July 27, 2016.

4. Ibid.

5. Frank Langfitt, "Blacberry or Crackberry? A PDA Culture War," National Public Radio, January 12, 2005.

6. Adam Thierer, "Bye Bye BlackBerry. How Long Will Apple Last?" Forbes.com, April 1, 2012.

7. Ibid.

8. John C. Dvorak, "Apple should pull the plug on the iPhone," *MarketWatch*, March 28, 2007, https://www.marketwatch.com/story/apple-should-pull-the-plug-on-the-iphone.

9. MacDailyNews, "RIM half-CEO doesn't see threat from Apple's iPhone," February 12, 2007.

10. Gregory Korte, "Through executive orders, Obama tests power as purchaser-in-chief," *USA Today*, October 11, 2015.

11. Andy Kessler, "Robots, 3-D Printers and Other Looming Innovations," *Wall Street Journal*, August 7, 2013.

12. Stewart Wolpin,"Commercial GPS Turns 25: How the Unwanted Military Tech Found Its True Calling," Mashable, May 25, 2014.

13. Steven F. Hayward, *The Age of Reagan: The Fall of the Old Liberal Order* (Roseville, Calif.: Forum, 2001), 290.

14. Ibid., 7.

15. "Wi-Fi Will Connect Them All," http://www.wi-fi.org/download.php?file=/sites/default/files/private/Infographic_15_Years_of_Wi-Fi_0.pdf

16. Hayward, *The Age of Reagan*, 31.

17. Greg Milner, *Pinpoint: How GPS Is Changing Technology, Culture, and Our Minds* (New York: Norton, 2016), xvi.

18. John Divine, "The $68B Uber IPO Is DEFINITELY Not Worth the Wait," InvestorPlace, April 19, 2016.

19. Konstantin Kakaes, "New Directions," *Wall Street Journal*, June 25–26, 2016.

20. Ludwig von Mises, *Socialism* (Indianapolis: Liberty Fund, 1979) translation of 2nd edition, 11.

21. "New immunotherapy drug behind Jimmy Carter's cancer cure," *The Guardian*, December 6, 2015.

22. Steven Kutz, "This dog walker probably makes more money than you do," *MarketWatch*, February 9, 2016.

23. Ibid.

24. Alexander Lobrano, "By the Numbers: The Ritz Paris," *New York Post*, July 26, 2016.

25. Todd Van Luling, "11 Things You Didn't Know About Costco," *Huffington Post*, February 7, 2014.

26. Source, GuildSomm, https://www.guildsomm.com/stay_current/discussion_ forums/f/109/t/7078.

27. Dan Neil, "Aston Martin Lagonda: The Thoroughbred Limo," *Wall Street Journal*, August 20–21, 2016.

28. Jo Piazza, "It Girl Inc.," *Marie Claire*, September 2016.

29. Julie Cresswell, "Young and in Love, With Lipstick and Eyeliner," *New York Times*, November 23, 2017.

30. Ibid.

31. Ibid.

32. Ibid.

Chapter Nine: Why We Need People with Money to Burn

1. Warren Brookes, *The Economy in Mind* (New York: Universe Books, 1982), p. 77.

2. Walter Isaacson, *Steve Jobs* (New York: Simon & Schuster, 2011), 407.

3. Ibid., 157.

4. David McCullough, *The Wright Brothers* (New York: Simon & Schuster, 2015), 34.

5. Ibid., 108.

6. Konstantin Kakaes, "New Directions," *Wall Street Journal*, June 25–26, 2016.

7. Isaacson, *Steve Jobs*, 339.

8. Dawn Kawamoto, Ben Heskett, and Mike Ricciuti, "Microsoft to invest $150 million in Apple," CNET, August 6, 1997.

9. Alexis Tsotsis, "Uber Gets $32 Million From Menlo Ventures, Jeff Bezos, and Goldman Sachs," *Tech Crunch*, December 7, 2011.

10. Source: Forbes, http://www.forbes.com/profile/jeff-bezos/.

11. Peter Thiel with Blake Masters, *Zero to One* (New York: Crown Business, 2014), 84.

12. Noam Cohen, "Technology's Trumpian Visions," *New York Times*, July 27, 2016.

13. Enrico Moretti, *The New Geography of Jobs* (New York: Houghton Mifflin, 2012), 37.

14. Ibid., 13.

15. Ibid., 168.

16. Ibid., 52.

17. Ibid., 60.

18. Ibid., 62.

19. Michael Freeman, *ESPN: The Uncensored History* (Lanham, Md.: Taylor Trade Publishing, 2000), 58.

20. Ibid., 59.

21. Ibid.

22. Ibid., 7.

23. Ibid., 77.

24. Thomas Kessner, *Capital City: New York City and the Men Behind Its Rise to Economic Dominance, 1860–1900* (New York: Simon & Schuster, 2003).

25. T. A. Heppenheimer, *Turbulent Skies: The History of Commercial Aviation* (Hoboken, N.J.: Wiley, 1995), 109.

26. Ibid., 111.

27. Ibid., 111–112.

28. Walter Isaacson, *The Innovators: How a Group of Hackers, Geniuses and Geeks Created the Digital Revolution* (New York: Simon & Schuster, 2014), 185.

29. Ibid., 186.

30. Source, IMDB.com, http://www.imdb.com/name/nm2691892/?ref_=nv_sr_1.

31. Source, IMDB.com, http://www.imdb.com/name/nm3267061/?ref_=fn_al_nm_1.

32. Arthur Brooks, *Who Really Cares* (New York: Basic Books, 2012), 112.

33. George Gilder, *Knowledge and Power: The Information Theory of Capitalism and How It Is Revolutionizing the World* (Washington, DC: Regnery, 2013), 5.

34. Isaacson, *The Innovators*, 105.

35. Tim Harford, *Adapt: Why Success Always Starts with Failure* (New York: Farrar, Straus and Giroux, 2011), 10.

36. Source, ESPN Fact Sheet, http://espnmediazone.com/us/espn-inc-fact-sheet/.

37. Brooks, *Who Really Cares*, 101.

38. Ibid., 113.

39. Gilder, *Knowledge and Power*, 180.

Chapter Ten: Love Your Robot, Love Your Job

1. Russell Banks, "20 Odd Questions," *Wall Street Journal*, July 30–31, 2016.

2. Andre Agassi, *Open* (New York: Alfred A. Knopf, 2009), 13.

3. Henry Hazlitt, *Economics in One Lesson* (New York: Three Rivers Press, 1979), 28.

4. Source: Forbes, Highest Paid Athletes, http://www.forbes.com/athletes/list/#tab:overall.

5. Source: Forbes, Highest Paid Celebrities, http://www.forbes.com/celebrities/list/#tab:overall.

6. Source: Forbes, The World's Billionaires, http://www.forbes.com/billionaires/list/.

7. Joel Trammell, *The CEO Tightrope* (Austin: Greenleaf Book Group Press, 2014), 79.

8. Mat Smith, "Meet the laundry-folding washing machine of our lazy-ass future," Engadget, October 7, 2015.

9. Enrico Moretti, *The New Geography of Jobs* (New York: Houghton Mifflin Harcourt, 2012), 36.

10. Eric John Abrahamson, *Building Home: Howard F. Ahmanson and the Politics of the American Dream* (Berkeley: University of California Press, 2013), 29.

11. Robyn Meredith, *The Elephant and the Dragon* (New York: Norton, 2007), 59.

12. Hazlitt, *Economics in One Lesson*, 188.

13. Ibid., 188.

14. Ibid.

Chapter Eleven: Come Inside and Turn on the Xbox, You Have Work to Do

1. Alexandra Wolfe, "Weekend Confidential: Phil Hellmuth," *Wall Street Journal*, August 12–13, 2017.

2. *USA Today*, Sportsline, May 26, 2015.

3. Stephanie Apstein, "Game of Throngs," *Sports Illustrated*, November 2, 2015.

4. Ibid.

5. Ibid.

6. Darren Davis, "Should College Students Get a Scholarship to Play Video Games?"*SeattleMet*, July 18, 2016

7. Apstein, "Game of Throngs."

8. Ibid.

9. Ibid.

10. Sarah Needleman, "Newest Job in Sports: Videogame Coach," *Wall Street Journal*, July 29, 2015.

11. Steve Williams, *Out of the Rough: Inside the Ropes with the World's Greatest Golfers* (New York: Viking Press, 2015), 42.

12. Ibid., 22.

13. Ibid.

14. Ibid., 11.

15. Michael Bamberger, "King Among Us," *Sports Illustrated*, October 3, 2016.

16. Ibid., 14.

17. Ibid., 15.

18. Ibid., 24.

19. Ibid., 32–33.

20. Ibid., 33.

21. Ibid., 21.

22. Ibid., 187.

23. Hank Haney, *The Big Miss* (New York: Crown Archetype, 2012), 13.

24. Ibid., 20.

25. Ibid.

26. Ibid.

27. Ibid.,16–17.

28. Ibid., 54.

29. Ibid., 22.

30. Albert Chen and Will Green, "Mutual Attraction," *Sports Illustrated*, June 27, 2016.

31. Ibid.

32. "At Thanksgiving, Pet Owners Just Can't Say 'No' to Fido," *Wall Street Journal*, November 24, 2015.

33. Laura Meckler and Stephanie Armour, "For Pets, It's Fat Thursday with Pies, Dressing Under the Table," *Wall Street Journal*, November 25, 2015.

34. Choe Sang-Hun, "As Markets Spring Up, Leader's Grip on North Korea Slackens," *New York Times*, May 1, 2017.

35. Georgia Pellegrini, "Out of His Shell," *Wall Street Journal*, May 28–29, 2016.

Index